A TIMELESS CLAS

THE EVOLUTIO
OF MACHIN'S ICON

A TIMELESS CLASSIC

THE EVOLUTION
OF MACHIN'S ICON

Douglas N. Muir

THE BRITISH
POSTAL
MUSEUM
& ARCHIVE

Published by the British Postal Museum & Archive

2007

First published 2007
British Postal Museum & Archive
Freeling House
Phoenix Place
London WC1X 0DL
www.postalheritage.org.uk

ISBN 978-0-9553569-1-9

Designed by Colin Goodhew, Lucid Design, London
Manufactured in the EU by L.P.P.S. Ltd, Wellingborough, Northants NN8 3PJ

Acknowledgements to Royal Mail for assistance in the production of this book.
www.royalmail.com/stamps

CONTENTS

ACKNOWLEDGEMENTS

No book is the work of one person alone. Without the considerable help of others this one would not have been possible. I am particularly grateful to Tony Benn for giving permission to quote extensively from his published diaries and providing the Foreword, despite being very busy at the time. David Gentleman has given a great deal of assistance with regard to his involvement in the revolution in British stamp design in the mid 1960s. He has also read most of the text, making a number of very useful suggestions, and I am indebted to him for writing the Introduction.

Over a period of many years Francis Machin, Arnold Machin's son, has been unfailingly helpful - always finding yet more photographs, or correspondence and making plaster casts and sketches immediately available. Many of the illustrations in this book come from his archive and are published here for the first time. I am also very grateful to Francis for the personal memoir of his father he has provided, which adds a more human touch.

At the Royal Mint I must thank Kevin Clancy and Graham Dyer for providing access to their collections and the minutes of the Royal Mint Advisory Committee, and allowing the reproduction of the relevant illustrations. Colleagues at the British Postal Museum & Archive and members of staff of the National Archives at Kew have helpfully made the various official files available. Don Staddon has checked the sections on how the stamps were produced, making several trenchant comments, in particular on how the casts were photographed. Jeffery Matthews kindly checked the final section where he was involved in the project to replace the Machin design, and Graham Watson read the whole text with a view to making it less tedious. The index has been provided by Dr Jean Alexander. I am grateful to them all. Nevertheless, any errors of omission or commission are clearly my own.

However, my main debt is to Arnold Machin. Without his great work there would be nothing to write about, and the stamp and design worlds would be infinitely poorer. I do wish, though, that he had kept a voluminous day book at the time! Many questions still remaining might then have been answered.

A note on sources

Sources are given at the end of each chapter for all quotations. Those public record files with the department code POST are held by the British Postal Museum & Archive (as are those with the initials P, MD, and MKD – at the time of writing uncatalogued). Files with the code MINT are held by the National Archives at Kew. Published material has the author in bold type.

Illustrations

Unless otherwise stated, illustrations are copyright Royal Mail Group 2007 and are reproduced from the collections of the British Postal Museum & Archive. Two of the illustrations are from the Royal Philatelic Collection provided by the Keeper, Michael Sefi, and are reproduced by gracious permission of Her Majesty The Queen to whom copyright belongs, as does one other image. All credits are listed on page 236.

Douglas N Muir
March 2007

FOREWORD

BY TONY BENN

POSTMASTER GENERAL 1964-66

My first memories of the Post Office go back to the early thirties when my family used to go on holiday near a farm in Essex. Every day the postman would cycle in with the letters in a bag and then take my brother or me on the back of his bike as he pedalled away for his next port of call.

It was at the Durham Miners Gala in 1964 that Harold Wilson, then Leader of the Opposition, told me that if Labour won the election he had in mind appointing me as his Postmaster General. That was why I began thinking about the possibility that the GPO should adopt a policy for the arts, including a new policy for postage stamps.

When as PMG, a few months later, I found myself in the office at St Martin's-le-Grand, with a statue of Rowland Hill just outside my window I decided to make it known that I would welcome new designs for postage stamps.

David Gentleman responded and I commissioned him to prepare an Album illustrating how such designs might look, which he did and, in talks with him it became clear that the Queen's Head presented a design obstacle which required consideration.

The outcry against such a treacherous idea was immediate and my then recent battle to get out of the House of Lords led people to believe that the main motive was my republicanism, which was not the case.

This brilliant book by Douglas Muir at the British Postal Museum & Archive is primarily about the decision to commission a new head of the Queen by Arnold Machin, which I fully supported but it also deals with the story of the Head on the stamps in great detail.

I recorded it all in my diary including a hilarious audience with the Queen at Buckingham Palace where I showed her the Battle of Britain stamps, some difficult moments with the Stamp Advisory Committee and manoeuvring with the Civil Servants that would have provided the script for a "Yes Minister" TV series.

Even Harold Wilson found himself caught up in this Royal drama and the fact that Downing Street had been used to prevent any change indicated the extent of the threat as perceived by the advisers to the Crown, but it all ended happily.

British postage stamps were the first in the world, which is why, having the Sovereign's head on them, they are not marked "Great Britain" and they are widely admired for the wide-ranging subjects which they celebrate and for their imaginative designs.

From the very beginning of the penny post they have always aroused controversy, for on that occasion it was argued, by a dedicated Royalist, that it was inappropriate for people to lick the back of Queen Victoria's head before sticking it on a letter.

No-one seemed to comment on the fact that letters and packets which are taken to a local post office are franked with a mark "Royal Mail" and have no Head on them because all the publicity centred on the stamps themselves.

Minuscule art is highly specialised and by using it to depict our history, culture, industry, life and sporting activity a new way of telling the world all about Britain became possible which quickly caught on, became immensely popular and encouraged stamp collecting among a whole new generation.

The Post Office is being deliberately dismantled and replaced by a competitive system of collection and delivery under pressure from the European Union and those here who favour privatisation.

The role our stamps as a symbol of our national identity has therefore acquired a new significance, which gives this book a special importance.

INTRODUCTION

BY DAVID GENTLEMAN

When I was about seven or eight, an aunt gave me a stamp album for Christmas and a packet of assorted used stamps to stick in it. For a while I enjoyed this activity, finding out which countries had issued the stamps and sticking them in onto the right album pages with translucent hinges which came in a small tin box, itself hinged, like the ones that contained gramophone needles. I can remember a Liberian stamp because it was triangular and had an aeroplane on it,

1936 Liberia

1939 Switzerland

1935 Silver Jubilee
by Barnett Freedman

and I liked a as Swiss one with a bright white out of red cross. One of my favourites was a set of three double-sized stamps that had been issued a year or two earlier for the Silver Jubilee and designed by the artist Barnett Freedman, who was a friend of my father's.

But apart from them I didn't much like the British ones, which had no pictures on them to make them interesting to a small boy – only repetitive portraits, mostly of the faces of the same three kings, George V, Edward VIII and George VI. I certainly never had a Penny Black. And after a bit I gave up my stamp collection in favour first of matchbox covers with ships and tigers on them, and elastic bands that made them click shut; and then – during the war – in favour of a collection of bits of metal which I laid out on a bed of cotton wool. My school friends called these bits and pieces "souvenirs"; they were supposed to have come from German planes but they included tail fins from incendiary bombs and jagged shrapnel from the anti-aircraft shells which we heard banging in the night sky above us. After that I stopped collecting things altogether. I grew much more fascinated by the shapes of the planes that filled the skies than I had ever been either by stamps or matchbox tops or even "souvenirs", all of which I more or less forgot about.

So it was a surprise when, twenty years later and out of the blue, I was invited to enter a competition to design a set of three stamps for National Productivity Year. It seemed an unpromising subject; but, despite that, my designs of what I hoped were energetic and productive-looking arrows were chosen. This was

A TIMELESS CLASSIC

an unexpected stroke of luck. For although I had been earning my living as an illustrator and wood engraver for some years, I was still pretty inexperienced as a designer. After that, commissions for stamps for a Lifeboat conference and then a Shakespeare festival followed, and I began work on a Battle of Britain set. By then I'd grown familiar with the particular problems of designing stamps – or at any rate British ones – but I'd also realised that tradition and habit were so firmly embodied in the Post Office, and in its relationship with the monarchy, that these restrictive usages seemed impossible to dislodge.

1962 National Productivity Year – Gentleman's first stamp designs

But then Tony Benn became Postmaster General. One of the first things he did was to ask the general public to suggest ways of improving the quality of the design of British stamps. So I wrote to him proposing two things: firstly that stamp subjects should no longer be restricted to celebrating current events – not Shakespeare himself but a Shakespeare festival – but should reflect a wider view of everything British – history, architecture, the arts, engineering, nature; and secondly that on commemorative stamps (now called specials) the Queen's head should be left off and replaced by the words Great Britain or the initials UK. Benn was well-disposed to both these ideas and – bypassing and irritating the Stamp Advisory Committee and its eminent chairman Sir Kenneth Clark – he commissioned me to produce an album of a hundred stamp designs showing how such a programme would work and what it would look like it. My task included preparing designs for a new set of definitives retaining a new photographic portrait of the Queen. This idea was abandoned but it led eventually to the

commissioning of the Arnold Machin head which is the main subject of this book.

Machin's portrait has been used on all British definitives since then. It is a handsome work of great dignity: detailed yet capable of being well printed in photogravure, in a range of deep colours that allow its subtle modelling to read well when reduced to stamp size. It is a skilful and well-judged image to which continuous exposure has given iconic status.

Machin had taught at the Royal College of Art while I was a student there. He was attached to the School of Ceramics; I remember him as a senior figure, polite, unflamboyant but assured, with a distinguished-looking head which was bald on top but with flowing hair at the back. I had liked his Queen's ware bull for Wedgwood and admired him both as designer and craftsman.

This book is interesting, expert, well-researched and often amusing. It is devoted mainly to the history of Arnold Machin's portrait of the Queen. But in doing so it also touches on the time in the sixties when the brakes were taken off British stamp design. This change was not universally welcomed. Many people at the time who saw themselves as the guardians of time-honoured traditions were suspicious of it. The book shows how with some imaginative intervention from Tony Benn, the Postmaster General at the time, the Post Office despite its own misgivings came to accept change in a timid, blinkered and reverential stamp-issuing policy that had grown out of date.

Douglas Muir tells a good story fairly and dispassionately. I read it with interest as a reminder of the year or so in the mid-sixties when stamps briefly became my major preoccupation. Designing new ones, in ways which had previously been ruled out, was fun; and it taught me a lot – not just about squeezing pictures and ideas into a small space, but about design and determination, and how improbable things could be made to happen. Things were very different then. The Post Office was a large and self-confident department of the government (the Postmaster General was a minister) and run by cautious civil servants. Now it is – like most other European post offices – a semi-privatised, commercial organisation which has to make a profit to stay afloat. This book traces the early stages of this sometimes uneasy transition with insight and sympathy.

A TIMELESS CLASSIC

1

THE PENNY BLACK –
A SIMILAR CHALLENGE

The story of the iconic design featuring Queen Elizabeth II on present British stamps begins with the story of the Penny Black. That could be said of all postage stamps, but it is particularly true of the Machin design. Arnold Machin strove to recapture the simplicity, elegance and authority of the world's first stamp, some 125 years later.

 It is interesting to note that despite all the problems associated with being first in a completely new field, the Penny Black was conceived, designed, engraved, printed and put on sale, all in the space of five months, from January to May 1840. The design was deceptively simple. Rowland Hill had stated before (with regard to security from fraudulent imitation) that "there is nothing in which minute differences of execution are so readily detected as in a representation of the human face. .. I would therefore advise that .. a head of the Queen by one of our first artists should be introduced" [1]. Other security devices and value were added, but no country name. With no other rival, there was no need. This privilege of the monarch alone representing the United Kingdom on stamps has remained to this day, unique in the world.

There are other points of immediate comparison. The dimensions of the stamp have remained almost exactly the same for standard definitives for over 160 years, and the monarch is still normally the main feature, always facing left, or into the envelope. In this it differs sharply from coinage, where monarchs face in the opposite direction to their predecessor (Edward VIII being the typical exception). And it is interesting that both Queen Victoria and Queen Elizabeth are portrayed wearing the same diadem.

William Wyon

In 1840 the model of the head of Queen Victoria already existed. Created in 1838 by William Wyon, the greatest medallist of the day, it adorned the "City" medal commem-orating the visit of the young queen to the City of London in November 1837. However, this was based on a sketch originally drawn in 1834 when Princess Victoria was only 15. All British postage stamps were to have a portrait based on this throughout Victoria's long reign.

When, in 1839, Rowland Hill reported on the results of the Treasury Competition to devise methods of prepayment of postage he wrote that the stamp should be "as beautiful a specimen of fine art as can be obtained". In full, he said:

"There is nothing in which minute differences of execution are so readily detected as in a representation of the human face. ... I would therefore advise that either in the embossed or in the engraved part of the Stamp or perhaps in both, a head of the Queen by one of our first artists should be introduced; the best course to adopt would probably be to employ Mr Wyon to execute a die from which the embossed impression would be obtained, and from which, by means of Mr Bate's machine an engraved plate might also be made. By the use of the powerful press at the Mint, exact facsimiles of the die might be obtained in any number, and by a process somewhat similar, the engraved plate might also be multiplied without limit." [2]

Wyon was also Chief Engraver at the Royal Mint.

Creation of the Design

Without any tendering process Rowland Hill and Henry Cole came to an agreement with the security printers Perkins, Bacon and Petch that they should prepare a die "to be composed of the best Engraving of Her Majesty's Portrait which we can get executed by the best Artist, to be surrounded by white and black line Engine-turned work".[3] Hill confirmed that the Queen's head was to be drawn from Wyon's City medal.

Drawing by Henry Corbould based on the Wyon medal
Royal Philatelic Collection

The printers commissioned Henry Corbould to make a drawing from Wyon's medal and a sketch was submitted to Hill at the end of December 1839. Various detailed amendments were agreed extending the height of the design to its final size, adding corner decorations and variable lettering. Sheet size was determined at 240 (12 x 20) making the total value of one sheet of stamps £1.

Proofs from first die engraved — Ground work only

Stock engine-turning was transferred by Perkins, Bacon & Petch on to a die and an area was cleared for the engraving of the head. This die, together with Corbould's sketch, was then given to Charles Heath for the head to be engraved, although it is likely that it was his son Frederick who carried out the work. However, the first die was a failure as it was too light to transfer and so in mid

Colour proofs of the experimental die for the Penny Black before the engraving of the head *Philbrick Collection*

January 1840 a new die was begun. By 20 February 1840 it was complete bar the corners and a proof was sent to Queen Victoria for her approval. Shortly afterwards Hill wrote to the printers saying that the Chancellor of the Exchequer (Francis Baring) had shown him an autograph letter from the Queen expressing her "high appreciation" of the stamp. [4]

Production

The beginning of March saw the engraving on the die of the agreed legend (POSTAGE/ONE PENNY) and of the decorative crosses in the upper corners. In the lower corners (left blank on the die) were to be variable letters as a further deterrent to forgery. After the image on the die had been transferred to the plate the corner letters at the bottom were punched in by hand on each of the 240 images.

OLD ORIGINAL.

Printing took place from 15 April at the works of Perkins, Bacon & Petch in Whitefriars Street, London. There were five (later six) flat-bed printing presses worked by a large diameter hand wheel, each press being capable of printing some 800 sheets of stamps in 24 hours. Before printing the sheets had to be dampened. Afterwards they had to dry and then be

THE PRINTING PRESSES USED FOR THE STAMPS.

gummed. There were, of course, no perforations at this time and so labels had to be individually cut from the sheet by scissors.

The first stamps (then termed "labels"), and also postal stationery, were put on sale in London on 1 May and became valid for postage on 6 May. By 10 May Rowland Hill recorded that "the demand for labels is such that the contractors (Perkins Bacon), though they now have five presses, are obliged to work night and day; they are now producing 600,000 (stamps) daily." [5]

Over a period of eight months there were 11 plates used, from which over 68 million Penny Blacks were printed. There was of course also a second value, the Twopence Blue, as well as the postal stationery designed by William Mulready, although the latter was much ridiculed and had to be withdrawn.

As can be seen there was no designer of the stamp. Rather it came about as a result of co-operation between master craftsmen at the printers, the engraver and Rowland Hill (on behalf of the Treasury rather than the Post Office). Nevertheless, the speed with which the challenge of creating the world's first adhesive postage stamp was met is quite remarkable, and the end result is arguably still the most beautiful example.

Later designs

In essence, the Penny Black design lasted for 40 years. Later Victorian stamps all bore the same portrait of the Queen and subsequent monarchs adopted very much the same format, if never achieving the same classical beauty. Printing processes changed and designs became more fussy. A radical change took place in 1936 with the stamps of King Edward VIII which were based simply on a photograph of the monarch and printed in photogravure, but this was of course short-lived and very controversial at the time.

Although the gravure process continued to be used in the reigns of King George VI and Queen Elizabeth II the designs were much more decorative, with symbols reflecting the various countries of the United Kingdom.

1   **Muir, D.N.** *Postal Reform & the Penny Black: A New Appreciation* 1990, p 97

2   ibid

3   **Bacon, E.D.** *The Line-Engraved Postage Stamps of Great Britain Printed by Perkins, Bacon & Co.,* 1920, Vol. II, pp. 21/2.

4   ibid p30

5   POST 100/1 Rowland Hill diary

2

A PORTRAIT WITH PROBLEMS

The first stamps of the reign of Queen Elizabeth II used a three-quarter photograph by Dorothy Wilding within frames incorporating regional symbols. This youthful portrait was also used in all larger commemorative stamps and pictorial high values, but these were few in number. Until 1960 there were only 15 British pictorial or commemorative stamps of the reign. Thereafter, the pace began to increase, if but slowly. Four stamps appeared in 1960; seven in 1961. With the increase in numbers came an increase in complaints from designers about the three-quarter Wilding photograph which had to be a dominant feature of the design and which had appeared on all British stamps since 1952.

Portrait by Dorothy Wilding after the diadem had been retouched

The Wilding photograph

A preliminary photographic sitting by Dorothy Wilding took place at Clarence House on 26 February 1952, almost three weeks after the death of The Queen's father, King George VI. Wilding was briefed beforehand by both Post Office and Royal Mint officials with their different requirements for stamps and coins.

From this session three-quarter profile photographs of The Queen wearing a tiara were used by artists for initial definitive stamp designs. However, from

a heraldic point of view, it was felt that she should be wearing a coronet and so a fresh photographic session took place on 15 April. In a brocade gown, with the sash and star of the Order of the Garter, The Queen now wore the diamond diadem made for George IV in the 1820s, designed to be worn outside a Cap of State. The new three-quarter photograph selected was approved by The Queen on 5 May but with the proviso that The Queen felt it showed the coronet too far back on her head. This was then altered in the retouching, which also clarified the outline of the diadem for reproducing at stamp size. The Wilding portrait was then incorporated into various frames for definitives and also applied to larger high value and commemorative designs.

For postal stationery, other effigies were created in profile, either directly from another Wilding photograph or indirectly through an image used on overseas coins. However, these were to have no bearing on future postage stamp developments.

Designers' complaints

Two designers in particular had complaints or reservations about the use of the Wilding portrait – Faith Jaques and Michael Goaman, though other successful designers concurred. Their complaints were summarised in April 1961 as being that the photograph could only be satisfactorily included if it were put into a frame. There were also problems, described as "insuperable", in deciding where the portrait should be cut off. "The photograph was essentially a studio portrait and it just would not fit in with other symbolic or pictorial elements."[1] Jaques and Goaman were asked to experiment to create a new profile.

When Jaques replied with rough sketches in September she added a detailed critique entitled "Some problems in designing commemorative postage stamps". She criticised the size of the existing portrait, the modelling and lack of contrast, and the difficulty in fitting it in to wildly irrelevant subject matter.

"Being literally a 'photographic likeness' certain problems arise. In our older stamps, particularly some Victorian ones, there is a strong sense of the Queen's head standing for the monarchy as a symbol rather than as a realistic portrait. This is because the heads were slightly classical & stylised in treatment. In my view this feeling of regality is lost with the head in its present form. If the head is more firmly stylised, & slightly smaller, it is much easier to 'marry' it with the dissimilar subject-matter of the rest of the stamp." [2]

Later, Goaman recorded his rather similar views.

"With the Coronation of Queen Elizabeth came the photographic three-quarter face portrait officially approved as the only one to be used on British G.P.O. issues. Whilst

"Being literally a 'photographic likeness' certain problems arise. In our older stamps, particularly some Victorian ones, there is a strong sense of the Queen's head standing for the monarchy as a symbol rather than as a realistic portrait."

Faith Jaques

an excellent study in many ways, it has created some of the objections to the use of the portrait to symbolise the country's name and the apparent difficulty of a 'personal photo' appearing in close juxtaposition with symbols or pictorial design. In the former case, because the portrait might not relate in style with the rest of the drawing, and in the latter, that the head could, to some eyes, appear incongruously as part of the picture. The other weakness of a half turned portrait is the mere fact that it looks outward and can occasionally create an unavoidable peep-show effect or that the subject matter has to be carefully chosen before putting it alongside this type of photograph." [3]

Years later, when Tony Benn first informed designers about his ideas, others added their own criticisms. M.C. Farrar Bell had always thought a three-quarter portrait a mistake. All the best stamps of the past had used a profile head.

"I feel a return to an 'effigy' head rather than another photograph would be better still. There is a certain rightness about an effigy for the small scale of a stamp. It also has the advantage of dating more slowly than a photograph." [4]

Reynolds Stone agreed, and went on to defend the use of a head.

"Not having the Monarch's Head would of course make the designer's job easier, but I can very much see the arguments in favour of keeping it. It makes our stamps unique, and is a permanent reminder that they were invented in this country." [5]

Experimental profile portraits

In September 1961 Faith Jaques produced a series of stamp-size sketches based on stamp designs up to that year. Into the existing frames she inserted a drawn profile image of The Queen. When the Stamp Advisory Committee of the Council of Industrial Design was considering designs for the 1963 Red Cross issue the problems of the use of the Wilding resurfaced. Referring to the Jaques' modified heads it was noted:

"The Committee thought them most satisfactory and asked if [the Post Office] would get some artists preparing a new head. Sir Kenneth [Clark] said artists would be quite capable of working from photographs and a sitting of the Queen would not be necessary. He would sound the Duke of Edinburgh about the Queen's reaction to a redesign of the approved head." [6]

Profile head by
Michael Goaman

No comment was made on the drawn head which had been submitted by Michael Goaman. This

Suggestions by
Faith Jaques to
show the effect of
a profile portrait

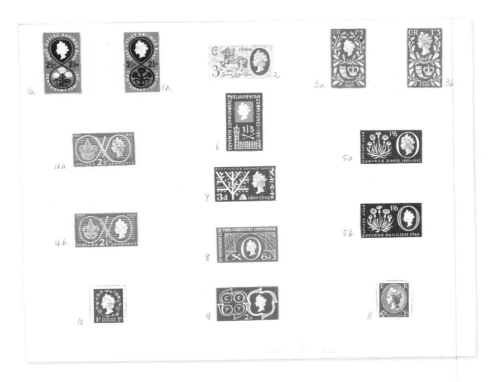

Goaman described as a "modified" likeness where the bone structure of the cheek had been emphasised to give a more clear-cut effect. [7] The Post Office had sent it to Harrisons, the stamp printers, for retouching and it had been returned "considerably improved" in February 1962. Goaman said he would like to experiment further but there is no evidence that he did. He did use his profile portrait on stamps, however. Later in the decade he submitted various designs for British stamp issues initially bearing it, and some were accepted on designs produced for the Crown Agents for colonial stamps.

Buckley photographs

As a result of Clark's "soundings" profile photographs of The Queen by Anthony Buckley were sent from the Palace to the Post Office, and thence the

Council of Industrial Design, in March 1963. These had recently been taken for use as the basis of stamp designs in the Commonwealth and were with and without tiara. Returning them Mrs Tomrley, the COID Stamp Advisory Committee co-ordinator, remarked that "the portraits perhaps err on the solemn side."

"If the effigy is to be a good portrait as well as a good design stamp-wise, it cannot I think just be a direct abstraction from a single photograph." [8]

When returning the photographs to the Palace Frank Langfield, a postal official, explained:

"We had in mind attempting a drawn head of Her Majesty to meet some artistic comment about the difficulties of marrying a photograph with a stamp design, but the photographs do not lend themselves particularly well to the making of a drawing and we have let the matter drop for the moment." [9]

1962. Photographic portraits by Anthony Buckley for use on stamps (with and without a tiara)

1 POST 122/10703 Postage Stamps. Stamp Design Policy. New look. Requests to Faith Jaques and Michael Goaman to experiment.

2 ibid

3 **Goaman, Michael** "Problems of Designing British Stamps" *Philatelic Bulletin* Vol. II, No. II December 1964.

4 POST 122/10710 Postage Stamps. Stamp Design Policy: New look. Correspondence with the Palace.

5 ibid

6 POST 122/10703 op cit

7 ibid

8 POST 122/10704 Postage Stamps. Stamp Design Policy: new look. Photographs loaned.

9 ibid 23 July 1963

3

ARNOLD MACHIN: MAN & SCULPTOR

Arnold Machin was born in the year the *Titanic* was launched and lived to the last year of the 20th century. Despite coming from a poor background he showed an early interest in, and gift for, art and this was encouraged. Throughout his life he fought for his view of art, largely decrying modern trends. He had a gift for publicity and controversy and could be difficult to satisfy until things were painstakingly just right.

Child Fishing watercolour by Arnold Machin, aged 6.

Born on 30 September 1911 to a poor family in Oak Hill, Stoke-on-Trent in the Potteries, Arnold was the ninth child of 12. From his earliest years he loved to draw and in his *Memoirs* he recounts how "the entire family would stint themselves to provide me with books, pencils, watercolours, scraps of paper and wrapping paper with which to work." [1] His earliest known work is a remarkably accomplished ink and watercolour sketch of a child fishing, produced when he was only five or six. By the time he was 14 he left school and began an apprenticeship at Minton, the famous porcelain manufacturer, learning to decorate china.

For a period during the Depression Machin was out of work and it was not until 1933 that he gained a job as painter and gilder at the Old China Works in Derby. While there he went to evening classes at the Derby School of Art, later becoming a full-time student in a course which included sculpture. From there, in 1937, he won a three-year scholarship to the Royal College of Art (RCA) in London to study sculpture under Professor Richard Garbe. During holidays he did part-time work which included helping Cecil Thomas (an old student of Garbe's) with modelling coats-of-arms.

"Amongst other things [Thomas] did a great deal of coinage designing, so that while I was working in his studio I was able to observe the techniques involved." [2]

At the RCA clay became Machin's medium and he dropped woodcarving and sculpture in marble to develop work in terracotta. He completed his scholarship in 1940 and was awarded the Silver Medal, the top award of the Royal College of Art. This included a travelling scholarship which he was unable to take up because of the outbreak of war.

Machin returned to Stoke as Head of Stoke Art School but soon joined Wedgwood as a designer. Josiah Wedgwood (the fifth of that name) wrote that "Machin's work as a modeller might be at least as much of an asset as [Eric] Ravilious' work as a designer." [3] Later he was both sympathetic and supportive when Machin, as a conscientious objector, was sentenced to 12 months in Wormwood Scrubs prison (serving nine).

As well as doing designs for Wedgwood he was free to do his own terracottas which they fired for him and stored at the factory. Two of these, *St John the Baptist* and the *Annunciation* group, were shown to John Rothenstein at the factory by the Wedgwood design Director and he purchased both pieces for the Tate Gallery, of which he was Director, in 1944.

In a letter to a former prison colleague Machin summed up some of his artistic ideas in response to comments about his terracottas.

"I agree with you in your dislike of naturalistic art when you use the term to describe a mere copy of surface forms without reference to the animated, abstract something which I suppose is the life or spirit of a being or thing. In a sense Epstein's portraits are naturalistic, so is the work of Donatello, M. Angelo & Dürer since they express themselves with natural forms. The immortal quality of their work, however, is the result of a profound understanding of the hidden forms or abstractions of life, though they must use a language which is understandable in order to convey their ideas to others. The indefinable must be expressed in a concrete form. To quote from the Bible, 'the word must be made flesh', which I think is an extremely lucid phrase and describes what I mean admirably." [4]

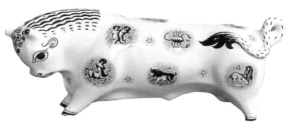

Taurus Wedgwood 1945, Queen's ware decorated with lithographed zodiac patterns

On his return to the Potteries he was appointed a full-time figure modeller at Wedgwood where he designed a bull which could be simply modelled and decorated with lithographs by wartime unskilled labour. *Taurus* was a great success and sold for over 30 years.

Shortly after the war it was suggested that he submit a terracotta figure for possible inclusion in the Royal Academy Summer Exhibition.

"I immediately set to work in my studio at 'The Lea' to produce a terracotta in the classical Italian style, much larger than I had ever attempted before. It was to be a seated nude, about 5 feet high, with attendant cherubs and entitled 'Spring'." [5]

After working on it for months it was taken to Wedgwood for firing, though this was almost a disaster as it broke in the kiln and the sculpture had to be painstakingly restored. Nevertheless, it was accepted for exhibition and later purchased by the Royal Academy under the Chantrey Bequest for £1,000, eventually going to the Tate Gallery. As a result of this Machin was elected an Associate of the Royal Academy in 1947.

At that year's Summer Exhibition Machin met Patricia Newton, an artist also exhibiting for the first time, whom he remembered from their days at the Derby Art School. Two years later in 1949 they were married; their son Francis was born in November and the family moved to "The Villas" in Stoke-on-

Trent. Arnold then became a part-time tutor at the RCA and combined this with work for Wedgwood.

Wedgwood portrait medallion of The Queen, early 1950s

In 1956 the city council proposed to remove the Victorian gas lamp standards in the street outside the Machin house and replace them with concrete posts and electric lighting. Arnold and Pat's protest made national newspaper headlines (and won accolades from John Betjeman and the Royal Institute of British Architects) as he chained himself to the central standard when workmen came to remove it.

"This is my protest against the destruction of all the beautiful things, which is going on in this country." 6

Arnold and Pat Machin and their protest about the Victorian gas lamp, 1956

The protest was defeated but attracted a great deal of attention and led to others making similar protests. However, the old lamp was kept and erected in his garden. Now replica Victorian lamps have replaced the concrete standards.

"When people worship old things it is not just sentimentality; there is a living force there which attracts and, whether they recognise

this or not, each hand-crafted object produces its own vitality which penetrates and has an effect on them." [7]

Machin was elected a full member of the Royal Academy in 1956. In 1959 he was elected Master of Sculpture in the Royal Academy Schools. His teaching involved about 15 students but he became depressed at the trends in modern art and sculpture. At this time he took over a spacious converted mews studio in Sydney Close in Chelsea.

In 1962 Machin was on the Council of the Royal Academy, with Sir Charles Wheeler as President. Because of financial difficulties it was decided to sell one of their possessions – Leonardo da Vinci's cartoon of *The Virgin and Child with St. Anne and St. John the Baptist*. This was something which Machin violently opposed and resulted in him dramatically resigning from the Council, though he remained as a teacher in the Schools for several years.

It was at this point that Machin was invited to take part in the competition for the design of the new decimal coinage discussed in the next chapter.

Later Life

Much of the next few years was taken up with the commissions to design British coinage and stamps, as detailed in later chapters. Other work included coins for the Bahamas, Guernsey, the UK Silver Jubilee crown and various medals such as the Michelangelo Medal of 1979 for the Royal Academy Trust Appeal, and the Churchill medal of 1965.

From the 1970s the making of gardens occupied most of Machin's leisure time, firstly at Offley Rock, Eccleshall in Staffordshire where he moved in 1957 and then Garmelow Manor nearby. A BBC film of the gardens at Offley Rock was made in 1977 by Norman Painting for the series "A Summer of Gardens".

Towards the end of his life he spoke out against the 1996 "Sensations" exhibition at the Royal Academy and all which that represented in trends in modern art. He spent his last two years writing his memoirs. In the last chapter he wrote:

"I am convinced that hard work is the key to success. So many people today are protected from reality and have become apathetic. I firmly believe that the secret of contentment is to accept what you have and to make the most of it — not stretching for the impossible but working to one's utmost for the possible." [8]

Girl in Hat 1940s. Figure by Machin recessed in the holly hedge at Offley Rock.

1   **Machin, A.** *Memoirs: Artist of an Icon* 2002 p11

2   ibid p60

3   *The Life and Times of Arnold Machin OBE, R.A.* exhibition catalogue Royal Academy Schools 2001, p9

4   *Memoirs* op cit p87

5   ibid p95

6   ibid p109

7   ibid p110

8   ibid p157

4

THE DEVELOPMENT OF A COIN EFFIGY

Three years before he was involved in the design of stamps Machin worked on an effigy of The Queen for the new, forthcoming decimal coinage. It was this which brought him to the attention of Sir Kenneth Clark and other members of the Stamp Advisory Committee when they were thinking about a new profile on stamps. There were many parallels in the story of the development of the coin design with that of the subsequent stamps. Much of the origination was, at least initially, the same and many personalities appear in both stories. Machin's experience with the modelling of the coin effigy influenced and helped him when it came to the stamps. A study of how the coins came about illuminates and explains a great deal of what happened later. This chapter concentrates on Machin's contribution to the process.

First Thoughts

The question of decimal coinage was first discussed by the Royal Mint Advisory Committee (on the design of coins, medals, seals and decorations) as early as their meeting of 10 April 1962, even though decimalisation was still almost a decade away, and not yet publicly announced. This committee was headed by the Duke of Edinburgh as President and, apart from the Deputy Master of the Mint (J H James – Chairman), it included such luminaries from the arts as Sir Kenneth Clark, Francis Meynell, Milner Gray, Robert (Robin) Darwin and John Betjeman. Appointments to it are on the recommendation of the Master of the Mint (the Chancellor of the Exchequer) and approved by The Queen. Interestingly, two who were on the Committee at the time were also members of the Council of Industrial

Design's Stamp Advisory Committee (Clark and Gray) and Meynell had until recently been Typographical Advisor to the Postmaster General for many years.

Clearly, the presence on the Committee of the Duke of Edinburgh was both highly influential and helpful in providing access to The Queen and her views, especially in the matter of her image. Right from the outset the Duke declared that the effigy should be changed from the current head by Mrs Mary Gillick in order to distinguish the new coinage from the old. He also preferred "a tiara to the diadem because the latter is on the stamps and banknotes already." [1] Although the Gillick head was still relatively new, only having been in use for some nine years at this point, there were also some technical aspects of wear of those coins which meant that a new model would be desirable.

Design Teams

It was decided that there should be competing teams of designers. These were invited from various institutes - the Royal Institute of British Architects (R.I.B.A.), the Royal Academy and the Faculty of Royal Designers for Industry (R.D.I.). The last later combined resources with the Royal College of Art (R.C.A.). Approved photographs by Anthony Buckley were supplied to the Royal Mint in August. These had already been approved for use on postage stamps (appearing on definitives for Australia and Bahamas and other Commonwealth stamps), and as mentioned earlier were also supplied to the British Post Office for that same purpose (see page 19).

At the end of August 1962 Sir Charles Wheeler, President of the Royal Academy, arranged for submissions from the Royal Academy. There is no reference to this in the RA Archives and it seems to have been on the basis of friends of his, or fellow council members. He wrote to Machin:

"The Mint is seeking new Coinage designs & has asked me to get three members to submit sketches. Would you be willing to be one of them - the others will be McMillan and myself? There will be a small fee in the first place." [2]

All of these were sculptors. McMillan had been Master of Sculpture at the RA from 1929 to 1941 and Machin was currently in that post, and on the Council.

The most formally organised team was that of the R.C.A./R.D.I. At the beginning of October 1962 Milner Gray invited various artists to submit designs for both the obverse and reverse of the coins. They were: Ronald Armstrong, Robert Goodden, Geoffrey Clarke, Reynolds Stone, Richard Guyatt and Christopher Ironside, though not all prepared drawings. Also on the team were Robin Darwin and two advisors — John Pope-Hennessy of the Victoria & Albert Museum, and Stanley Morison of typography fame from *The Times*. [3]

Drawings submitted

Three unattributed batches of drawings were delivered from the Royal Academy to the Royal Mint on 29 November, to be followed the next day by two sets of designs by Edward Bawden and Andrew Anderson of the Royal Institute of British Architects. These were considered at the next meeting of the Royal Mint Advisory Committee which was on 10 December. For the various designs required for the reverse of the coins it was agreed that two artists should be asked to develop their sketches — Edward Bawden and Christopher Ironside. However, Sir Kenneth Clark suggested that it might be worthwhile asking Machin to develop "one or two" of his designs to a plaster stage.

"In their present form the designs appeared to be more suitable for repoussé silver work than for coinage, but they had been submitted only as rough sketches and appearances might be deceptive." [4]

Reverses by Mr. A. Machin

May 1963.
Photographs of
plaster casts for
reverse designs by
Machin as seen and
rejected by the
Royal Mint Advisory
Committee.

Detailed comments were made on the heraldry of Machin's designs and, in the end, Machin submitted a total of seven designs for reverses in plaster cast form. However, versions by Christopher Ironside were preferred.

With regard to the obverse design it was agreed that The Queen's "portrait must be indisputably the chief element of the design and that the inscription should accordingly be given as little prominence as possible". [5] Bawden and Ironside were to produce further drawings but

"Mr Machin's sketches indicated that he possessed the sort of talent required for a coinage portrait and that he also should be invited to progress an obverse design." [6]

"In their present form the designs appeared to be more suitable for repoussé silver work than for coinage, but they had been submitted only as rough sketches and appearances might be deceptive."

Fully developed drawings were required by the end of January 1963, though artists should consider themselves free to produce "models" if they so wished.

Snowdon photographs

Robin Darwin pointed out that the Buckley photographs as supplied to artists were not entirely satisfactory and wondered if Lord Snowdon might be asked to help. Prince Philip (President) agreed that this should be done, and it was arranged that Snowdon would take further photographs over Christmas [7]. In his *Memoirs* Arnold described a scene where the remaining competitors met Snowdon at the Royal College of Art (on 19 December [8]) to brief him on their requirements.

Some of the still
photographs taken
by Lord Snowdon,
Christmas 1962,
used as a basis for
both coin and
stamp designs.

A TIMELESS CLASSIC

A TIMELESS CLASSIC

A TIMELESS CLASSIC

Sketch drawings by
Machin based on
the Snowdon
photographs.

A TIMELESS CLASSIC

"I asked him if I could have a series of photographs of The Queen taken at every angle from the front of her head to the back, with The Queen seated on a revolving chair." [9]

This would seem to be the origin of the 16mm film taken by Snowdon with the various still photographs both with and without tiara (but not diadem - important for subsequent events). It is not clear precisely when this was made but it was presumably over Christmas 1962 as arranged. Machin was informed on 1 January that the head should be "uncrowned but may have a tiara or a diadem". [10] To that end prints of a 1952 Wilding photograph of The Queen facing left and wearing the diadem were sent to Machin on 8 January, but he preferred to work on models without.

First relief

Designs were required by 28 January 1963 as the Committee next met on the 29th. However, this was the very severe winter of 1962-63 when much of the countryside came to a standstill for several weeks. Machin wrote in manuscript to explain his difficulties to Alan Dowling, Secretary of the Committee:

"Unfortunately I shall not be able to complete the lettering for my design of the Queen's effigy for the new coinage before the committee meeting on Tuesday.

The extremely severe weather we have endured since before Christmas with all the problems of being snowed up over a long period together with various illnesses in the family made it impossible to get the lettering completed.

However, I have completed the effigy in wax and the lettering which I intend to form in an unbroken band round it would present no problems should my design be chosen.

I would be grateful if you would explain this to the committee. Although I prefer the effigy without the tiara and necklace I would of course be prepared to incorporate them in the design if this was desired." [11]

The original wax effigy with traces of lettering still exists. Five days later a formal typed letter followed accompanying the plaster moulds. Lettering was still not complete but was pencilled in.

"I am submitting two effigies of the Queen because I prefer the one without the tiara and necklace. However, if it is compulsory to incorporate the jewels in the design, I should point out that further work is required to relate the head properly to the tiara, which as you will see is only indicated roughly." [12]

At their meeting the following day the Committee considered three obverse treatments by Bawden, Ironside and Machin. They preferred the two with tiaras – a watercolour by Ironside and one of the moulds by Machin. However, members "agreed with Sir Kenneth Clark that the proportions of Mr Machin's preferred model were good and that the pose was both novel and attractive. ..."[13] This was the larger one without tiara and without any lettering. John Betjeman liked the design which he described as having more movement than the others, though he thought the style somewhat "sugary".[14] There was a suggestion that other tiaras might be more suitable, a "spiky" version being mentioned.

An undated internal memo prepared for discussion with Machin at this time mentioned that the inscription should be split into two halves as in a design by Ironside. The "sly" look of The Queen should be avoided and the portrait seemed to be over-modelled.[15] This last criticism continued throughout later discussions but was in the end regarded by Sir Kenneth Clark as a benefit as it worked better in the smaller size of coins.

29 January 1963. Photographs of Machin's two effigies (with and without tiara) as seen by the Royal Mint Advisory Committee.

Later models

Photographs and the Committee's comments were sent to Machin in March and he was asked to produce another portrait model at least one week before their next meeting which was on 15 May. Interestingly, the question of fees now came up and Dowling offered £750 for this stage of the work after the meeting of 29 January. This was to cover any work including sittings required to translate his model into a satisfactory coinage die. A fee of £1,000 was sent to Wheeler for all the work of the Royal Academy up to the end of January. In his *Memoirs* Machin mentions a fee of £300 for the competition which Wheeler "insisted on having .. for himself and William McMillan, saying that I had the job and the prestige!"[16] Machin made no mention of subsequent fees. From now on, the idea of competing teams was dropped and work continued with the individual artists.

For their May meeting Machin produced a series of seven different versions labelled A to G, and these were compared with a set by Ironside.

"The President said that he found neither set of designs very like The Queen, but he thought Mr Ironside's designs lacked distinction, and were rather wooden. ... he liked Mr

16 May 1963. Series of seven obverses by Machin seen by the Royal Mint Advisory Committee (C was preferred).

A TIMELESS CLASSIC

Machin's treatment of the shoulders and thought C the most human of his designs. Mr Betjeman admired Mr Machin's designs and thought them rather beautiful. They carried the stamp of a portrait artist." [17]

Committee members liked Machin's style of lettering. Machin heard later that John Betjeman had thought he had "made her look a bit sexy." [18] They now wanted a further plaster from personal sittings using design C as a basis. Prince Philip undertook to arrange this with The Queen. Despite previous suggestions the "spiky" tiara in version D was not liked, being compared to a railing.

Personal sittings

Personal sittings were arranged with The Queen at Buckingham Palace, where Machin made a series of drawings of her head followed by modelling in relief with clay. These were arranged for early June and Martin Charteris (the Queen's Assistant Private Secretary) wrote to confirm the details.

"The Queen will be pleased to give you sittings at 2.30 p.m. on Thursday, 6th June and at 12 noon on Tuesday, 11th June. I will arrange for both sittings to take place in the Yellow Drawing Room where the stand and an easel will be available for you. I will ask The Queen to wear an off-the-shoulders dress and the tiara which figures in the majority of your preliminary studies." [19]

Before he went there Charteris wrote to Machin with Prince Philip's detailed views.

"I remember the day that Her Majesty had a trayful of tiaras brought in so that one might be chosen to be included in the portrait. She put them on, one after the other, asking which I liked best — that was really quite a thing to see. As it happened she liked one while I preferred another."

Arnold Machin, OBE

"His Royal Highness, and I believe also the other members of the Committee, definitely liked the general arrangement of design 'C' best. He has, however, stated specifically that the 'spiky' tiara is preferred. The question of which tiara is to be used is obviously one which you will have to discuss with The Queen at your first sitting. In the meantime I have asked Her Majesty to bring both tiaras with her to the sitting. It would, therefore, be possible for you to do work on both." [20]

According to Machin's *Memoirs* as promised different tiaras were provided.

"I remember the day that Her Majesty had a trayful of tiaras brought in so that one might be chosen to be included in the portrait. She put them on, one after the other, asking which I liked best – that was really quite a thing to see. As it happened she liked one while I preferred another." [21]

July 1963. Original mould (in reverse) based on life drawings, with three-quarter back profile.

The tiara used was not the "spiky" (Russian) one but rather one of festoons, scrolls and collet-spikes which had been given to The Queen as a wedding present by Queen Mary. Called the "Girls of Great Britain and Ireland" tiara it had been purchased from Garrard, the London jeweller, by a committee organised by Lady Eve Greville as a wedding present for the future Queen Mary in 1893. Described as a diamond festoon-and-scroll design surmounted by nine large oriental pearls on diamond spikes and set on a bandeau base of alternate round and lozenge collets between two plain bands of diamonds, it was normally worn by The Queen without the base or pearls. The tiara has appeared in many portraits of Queen Elizabeth II, including those featured on British, Australian, Jamaican and Ceylonese currency.

Trying to produce a true likeness did not seem to result in an acceptable coin design. The next model, showing rather more of The Queen's back, was not liked. At the Royal Mint Advisory Committee's meeting on 23 July members thought the new effigy a retrograde step.

23 July 1963.
The three-quarter
back profile effigy
as seen, and not
liked, by the Royal
Mint Advisory
Committee.

<u>DECIMAL COINAGE</u>

OBVERSE MODEL BY MR. ARNOLD MACHIN

Size of largest coin

Size of smallest coin

"Although in some ways it had caught a natural and recognisable expression, it lacked the poise of the earlier model, and some features particularly the jaw bone and the muscles in the neck were quite wrong. There was also something wrong with the treatment of the eye. The President said that the earlier model came very close to what was wanted and he would himself be happy to recommend it if nothing better could be done. If however Mr Machin thought he could improve upon it he was sure that Her Majesty would if necessary grant another sitting. Mr Machin should be told to preserve the pose of the original model but to try to improve the expression, particularly about the mouth." [22]

The further sitting necessitated Machin's travelling up to Balmoral in August when it was announced that The Queen was expecting a fourth child. On his return he, a vegetarian, was thanked with the present of a brace of grouse from the estate.

Final version

November 1963. Original mould for the final effigy for coins.

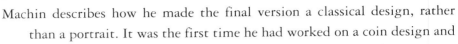

Machin describes how he made the final version a classical design, rather than a portrait. It was the first time he had worked on a coin design and he found it a challenging technique. The problem was to get the relief levels correct. "You have to make a depression where the ear comes, because that is normally the highest point, and then you work back from there." [23]

Milner Gray then produced tracings for the lettering, which was co-ordinated with Sir Francis Meynell. At the next meeting of the Committee on 5 November Machin was asked to attend. His latest effigy (without any lettering) in many ways reverted to the previous type "C".

November 1963. Original plaster cast for the final coin effigy.

It had been photographed lit from different directions for members to consider and a reduction punch in brass produced. Although some detail on the chin still required work "the Committee agreed that Mr Machin had achieved a very satisfactory design… [They] asked that their appreciation of the good work done by the artist should be recorded." [24]

5 November 1963.
Final coin effigy as
seen by the Royal
Mint Advisory
Committee.

Item 7 DECIMAL COINAGE DESIGNS

OBVERSE BY MR. ARNOLD MACHIN

ONE MODEL - LIT FROM DIFFERENT DIRECTIONS

Thereafter, the lettering needed to be added following his previous design and an electrotype of the whole produced by Walter Newman, Chief Engineer of the Mint. Machin personally supervised the final engraving in the dies at the Royal Mint at Tower Hill in the early part of 1964. Minor amendments were made to the hair and the details of the tiara and a third series of trial strikes were considered on 29 April. By this time doubts had set in and Machin wondered if the previous strikes had not been better.

Prince Philip's forthright views come clearly through the official, formal minutes:

"The President said that he did not share Mr Machin's doubts and felt that the design was now entirely satisfactory. In contrast with earlier strikes there was no part of the design that now caught the eye. The Committee agreed and endorsed the President's

suggestion that Mr Machin be heartily congratulated on his work and that this should be suitably recorded in the Minutes." [25]

When a press release was being prepared to announce the new coin design, Machin was asked to provide a summary of his aims.

"Designing the Coin – my aims by Mr Machin

"To produce a design with charm and dignity and yet without sentimentality.

"To create an illusion of strong relief thereby counteracting the stringent limits of the actual projection essential in Coin production.

To attempt to recapture something of the richness and vitality of the earlier British coins which has not seemed possible with the limiting techniques of modern mass production." [26] Much later, in retrospect, Machin defined the job of the coin designer as being "to produce a design which, when small scale and in low relief, can be reproduced in very large numbers, and which corresponds to the current concepts of representation. In modern times, when everyone knows what the monarch looks like, this has meant a naturalistic portrait." [27]

1968 proof 10p coin.

Machin's effigy was agreed for the obverse of the forthcoming coins and designs by Christopher Ironside for the reverses. When the results were announced, Ironside commented to Machin: "You're heads, and I'm tails!" [28] Interestingly, Ironside was also connected with stamps, designing at this time, with his brother Robin, the engraved high value Shakespeare stamp of 1964.

"Designing the Coin – my aims by Mr Machin

To produce a design with charm and dignity and yet without sentimentality.

To create an illusion of strong relief thereby counteracting the stringent limits of the actual projection essential in Coin production".

Arnold Machin, OBE

The new coin effigy was approved on 10 June 1964 by The Queen and Machin was awarded an O.B.E. for his work in March the following year. It was not until 1968 that the new coinage appeared in Britain, by which time the effigy had already been used elsewhere, in Southern Rhodesia and Australia.

Attention was now to turn to stamps.

1   MINT 20/3296 UK Decimal Coins – Advisory Committee – Use of teams

2   31 August 1962. letter from Sir Charles Wheeler to Machin

3   MINT 20/3296 op cit

4   ibid

5   ibid

6   ibid

7   11 December 1962. letter from Robin Darwin of RCA to Machin

8   ibid

9   **Machin, Arnold RA**, *Machin – Artist of an Icon* 2002 p131

10 MINT 20/3296 op cit

11 ibid

12 ibid

13 ibid

14 ibid

15 ibid

16 **Machin** op cit p134

17 MINT 20/3296 op cit

18 **Machin** op cit p 131

19 21 May, 1963. letter from Martin Charteris to Machin

20 MINT 20/3296 op cit

21 **Machin** op cit p 132

22 MINT 20/3317 Development of designs for decimal coinage

23 **Machin** op cit p132

24 MINT 20/3317 op cit

25 ibid

26 ibid

27 **Cook, Barrie** "Images of Royalty" *RA Magazine* No. 17 Winter 1987, p26

28 **Machin** op cit p131

5

"OFF WITH HER HEAD!"

Anthony Wedgwood Benn – official photograph as new Postmaster General, 1964.

It is ironic that the actions of a republican Postmaster General, intended to remove The Queen's head from stamps, should ultimately lead, instead, to the greatest regal icon of the 20th century. The revolution which took place in British stamp design and issuing policy in the mid 1960s resulted in the timeless sculpture of The Queen by Arnold Machin. Either the new Postmaster General brought a welcome breath of fresh air, or a devastating hurricane of change – it depended on your viewpoint at the time.

Tony Benn was appointed Postmaster General by Harold Wilson in the new Labour government of October 1964. Known then as Anthony Wedgwood Benn he arrived with definite and determined ideas about stamps, namely to try and remove The Queen's head from them (as well as widening their scope). As early as May 1963 he had mentioned this in a speech to a Labour Club in Oxford as a "mood-changing measure" on the advent of a Labour government. [1] Famous for his fight for the right to renounce an inherited peerage, and the first to do so, he was at the time a covert republican.

He had not been in office a month when he informed his shocked senior officials that he wanted commemorative issues without The Queen's head. In his diaries he remarked that "Obviously it is going to be necessary at some stage to declare myself openly as a republican and see what happens." [2]

Not yet, but he kept the initiative, informing a meeting of the Post Office Board on 25 November of new criteria for stamp issues:

"to celebrate events of national or international importance, to commemorate appropriate anniversaries and occasions, to reflect Britain's unique contribution to the arts and world affairs, to extend public patronage of the arts by promoting philately and to raise revenue." [3]

Only 10 months before, the *Philatelic Bulletin* (the GPO's new information sheet for stamp collectors) had felt able to announce, in lofty fashion:

"we receive many suggestions for [special stamp] issues and to keep their number within reasonable limits the policy of the Post Office is to confine them to marking outstanding national or international events and Royal and postal anniversaries. We do not mark anniversaries other than Royal and Postal ones nor do we issue stamps to support charities or other good causes.

"This policy does from time to time oblige us to refuse what could otherwise be eminently 'stamp-worthy' events. The history of Great Britain is however so rich in great occasions

"...if we were to attempt to depart from our policy we should either have a great increase in the number of special issues or, alternatively, be faced with the invidious task of discriminating between the many important historical events and notable personalities."

Philatelic Bulletin

and outstanding persons that if we were to attempt to depart from our policy we should either have a great increase in the number of special issues or, alternatively, be faced with the invidious task of discriminating between the many important historical events and notable personalities." [4]

The result had been stamps for various international congresses or festivals (Lifeboat, Red Cross, Geographical, Botanical and Shakespeare) which may have coincided with an anniversary, and National Productivity Year, Nature Week etc., but they were distinctly few in numbers. So the change now was dramatic and sudden.

Benn made his announcement in a written reply to a parliamentary question on 15 December and, referring to forthcoming 1965 issues, invited MPs and the public to submit suggestions to him as quickly as possible. After the announcement in the House of Commons Benn's new criteria were printed in the *Philatelic Bulletin*, slightly amended and omitting any mention of philatelic revenue, but repeating the public invitation for suggestions (stating that a large number had already been received).

Paul Reilly, of the Council of Industrial Design, and Sir Kenneth Clark, Chairman of the COID's Stamp Advisory Committee had a meeting with Benn on 13 January 1965, when he informed them of the proposed 1965 programme and that he wanted to establish a Fellowship in Minuscule Design. It was at this meeting that a new profile head of The Queen on definitives was first proposed. Discussion then continued about the design of commemorative stamps. Benn suggested that designers might have more scope if the stamp were designed "independently of the Queen's Head". Various ideas to achieve this were voiced. Minutes record:

*"At the end of the meeting it was agreed that all the people concerned would proceed at the greatest possible speed to get started on the May and June exercises, which would follow the conventional commemorative stamp pattern. For the later exercises in 1965 the new ideas mooted at this meeting would be tried out **so far as practicable**."* [5] *[author's emphasis]*

First Contact with David Gentleman

Undoubtedly, the most important suggestion from Benn's public invitation came with a letter from David Gentleman who already had a number of accepted stamp designs to his credit. Recently, Gentleman described what happened.

"By 1964 I'd already designed enough stamps to know what the problems were – mainly how to fit The Queen's head in alongside anything else – and had discovered ways of

coping with them. But I had also found out how immovable the Post Office's rules and usages were, particularly about this very subject. It was by a happy chance that Benn – determined, energetic, imaginative and eager for change – arrived just as I had become certain what these changes ought to be. So when he asked for suggestions I wrote to him proposing more interesting subject-matter and no Queen's head. This last suggestion was prompted not by any conscious republican leanings on my part but purely by considerations of what would work best as designs.

David Gentleman, c.1966

My letter to Benn took some weeks to work its way up through the doubtless disapproving Post Office machinery, and in the absence of any response I thought it must merely have been ignored as being too extreme and its proposals simply not on. But when it eventually got through to the PMG he rang me straight away to suggest a meeting. This was a surprise; the Post Office then was a rigid hierarchy, a vast pyramid with the PMG invisible at the top. The prospect of meeting him at all seemed a little alarming." [6]

In his original letter he wrote that he was convinced that "the main single drawback to the realisation of unified modern designs is the Monarch's head: not merely the unsatisfactory angle of the present photograph, but the traditional inclusion of the head at all." He continued:

"The problem is only in part one of insufficient space: it is essentially a problem of reconciling two conflicting elements and conventions within one design. In practice, the stamp design has to be split into two parts: the head and the rest. This can be managed with ingenuity, but, although interesting results are possible, they will always remain at best adequate and increasingly repetitive solutions to the same problem." [7]

The alternative could be a title which would be more adaptable and readily absorbed into the design "without as at present destroying it." Suggestions were UNITED KINGDOM, UK or GREAT BRITAIN.

This provided Benn with a great opportunity – to deal with The Queen's head from a design point of view, rather than politically. Dismissing the official, predictably negative, draft reply he telephoned Gentleman and asked him to come and see him.

"As far as I can remember [Gentleman writes] the first of these meetings was in the basement work-room of Benn's Holland Park house, early in the morning over a cornflake breakfast. I was a bit nervous, rather expecting to be overwhelmed. But the meeting was friendly and highly informal. And in contrast with my earlier talks with Post Office officials it was taken up with discussion not about what would be feasible or popular or acceptable to the Committee or to the Palace, but what was necessary and right.

Other meetings were in Benn's magnificently airy and spacious office at Post Office Headquarters in St Martin's le Grand. (But in the sixties even the relatively junior officials who had normally commissioned me had comparatively grand and high-ceilinged offices of their own in that large Edwardian building.) On occasion Benn came to my Camden Town studio." [8]

Thus began a unique co-operation between PMG and designer, and a lasting personal friendship. Often of like mind, the one was to inspire the other over 18 months of fervent, creative endeavour.

Churchill stamp

Sir Winston Churchill had died on Sunday, 24 January. Perhaps surprisingly, Benn felt this immediately as a shock.

"Thus ends the life of one of the greatest Englishmen of our time. Our family have much cause to be grateful to him. He it was who gave Father his extra twenty years of active

life in the House of Lords. Also he was one of those who supported me so much during my long constitutional struggle". [9]

By the next day he had decided he wanted a commemorative stamp. On his behalf the question of Churchill's head appearing beside that of The Queen was raised by Harold Wilson with The Queen at his next audience on 28 January. She approved, though Benn had already publicly announced that a stamp would be issued. At the same time postal officials had approached David Gentleman and invited him to submit designs quickly. Abram Games, a member of the Stamp Advisory Committee, and the printers Harrisons were also asked, designs to be ready by 10 February. The famous Karsh portrait of Churchill was to be used together with The Queen's head and the dates 1874 – 1965 (though these were later to be removed).

So it was that when Gentleman came to see Benn on 15 February he had already provided designs to the Post Office. Benn recorded that Gentleman had a Churchill stamp ready "with a tiny Queen's head on Churchill's massive shoulder and asked whether he could have the stamp reprinted without The Queen's head to see what it looked like. I said I could see no objection to this and that it would go before the Stamp Advisory Committee." [10] The SAC met the next day and Benn was furious to discover that Gentleman's design

Essay by the printers Harrisons with the Churchill portrait in combination with standard Wilding definitives.

Essay of Churchill design by Abram Games preferred by the SAC but rejected.

Essay of Gentleman's Churchill design without The Queen's portrait (replaced by Great Britain).

Essays of variations of Gentleman's accepted Churchill designs.

without The Queen's head had not been shown to them. Subsequently, at his insistence, essays were printed in this format.

At their meeting, the SAC strongly recommended one initial design by Gentleman together with that by Games, and two second choices (both by Gentleman). Later these were, exceptionally, shown to Lady Churchill who preferred the Committee's second choices. Benn also preferred the latter and recommended them to The Queen who approved this choice rather than the SAC's strong recommendations. As a result Abram Games demanded that his

The issued stamps with dividing white line

artwork be returned to him and, remarkably, this was agreed. In the accepted designs, detail about a white line dividing Queen from commoner, inserted in both Gentleman's designs rather than just the one as supplied, caused arguments with the designer and problems for the printers.

The final designs were sombre, but very effective, conveying Churchill's overwhelming contribution, and in so doing reducing The Queen's head to a small cameo in comparison.

Battle of Britain stamps & the Stamp Advisory Committee

When David Gentleman wrote his radical letter to the Postmaster General on 21 January he was already at work on designs for proposed stamps marking the 25th anniversary of the Battle of Britain. At his first meeting with Benn, as already noted, it was agreed that his Churchill design would be essayed without The Queen's head. Other than Benn's *Diary* there is no record of their conversation but it was clearly fruitful and Gentleman decided to use the Battle of Britain commission as an opportunity to experiment with these ideas: specifically the omission of The Queen's head from the outset, and the printing of stamp designs together in se-tenant blocks.

Perhaps significantly, there seem to be no minutes of the meeting of the Stamp Advisory Committee at which the resulting designs were first shown. The Stamp Advisory Committee (SAC) was under the auspices of the Council of Industrial Design, itself first set up in 1944 to be a centre of information and advice both for industry and government departments in matters of industrial art and design. Part of this remit was postage stamps (since 1945) and the present SAC was working to arrangements agreed in 1962, when Sir Kenneth Clark (already a member) became its Chairman. Since then the Committee's membership had been:

Sir Kenneth Clark, C.H., K.C.B. (Chairman)

Cecilia Lady Sempill A.R.C.A. Patron of the arts and writer on English pottery and china

James Fitton, R.A., F.S.I.A. painter and designer

Sir John Wilson Bt. K.C.V.O. – Keeper of the Royal Philatelic Collection

Milner Gray, R.D.I., F.S.I.A. industrial and graphic designer

Abram Games, O.B.E., F.S.I.A. – graphic designer of posters and stamps (including the Festival of Britain logo)

Professor Richard Guyatt, A.R.C.A. of the Royal College of Art

In the memorandum on relations between the COID and the Post Office the SAC's raison d'être was described:

"To assist the Postmaster General in selecting designs of British postage stamps which might be recommended to the Queen, the Council of Industrial Design will maintain a Stamp Advisory Committee. As its name indicates its role will be an advisory one." [11]

Advice would take the form of the names of artists to be invited to submit designs; the instructions to be sent to invited artists; and the designs to be selected for submission to The Queen.

However, "the Postmaster General will be free not to avail himself of the advice of this Committee, and to seek advice from any other quarter he thinks fit".[12] Understandably, this section was marked by Benn when he saw it. The PMG also reserved the right to submit to The Queen designs not recommended by the Committee.

Much later in the year a memo to Benn provides the Post Office's view of this committee:

"The Stamp Advisory Committee chooses designs according to the current concepts of commercial art and is inclined to put symbolism before pictorial presentation. The result is that many realistic and carefully prepared designs are summarily rejected, though in our view (and the printers') some of them would make excellent stamps. This has been pointed out by Post Office representatives, and Harrison's, at several Committee meetings, but no noticeable impact has been made on the Committee's attitude. The Committee has shown remarkably little interest in the possibility that its taste in design might differ from that of the people who use the stamps or collect them." [13]

Given these attitudes, and the personalities concerned, the reaction to Gentleman's revolutionary designs for the Battle of Britain stamps can be imagined. This was on 9 March and the events of that dramatic day were only recorded in a hand-written memo by Don Beaumont, a GPO official in charge of stamp production. [14] Designs by Andrew Restall had been with the Post Office for a week. Gentleman's designs were only delivered at 8.30 that morning for the SAC meeting at 9.30. There were 15 of his designs, 14 of which omitted The Queen's head. Beaumont did not comment on the omission of The Queen's head.

Gentleman also provided a synopsis to go with the designs. In February he had been warned by the Post Office about the politics surrounding the issue. Preference would be given to designs which were not too controversial, the

> *"The Committee has shown remarkably little interest in the possibility that its taste in design might differ from that of the people who use the stamps or collect them."*
>
> *Post Office memo*

Foreign Office having been against any issue at all. It was a time when the government wanted to be on good terms with the Germans in connection with possible entry to the E.E.C. and the Queen's forthcoming visit. Tactful handling was required and "flaming Heinkels etc" should be balanced by ack-ack batteries and fire over London with the familiar vapour trails of high flying aircraft.

In his synopsis Gentleman discussed at some length avoiding a controversial approach. He concentrated instead on the two types of plane most identified with the Battle of Britain — the Hurricane and the Spitfire.

"The familiar and acceptable convention of aircraft recognition silhouettes has therefore been developed purposely in these designs in order to tone down a too lurid or propaganda interpretation of what was, after all, the essential basis of the Battle of Britain — duels in the air.

In developing this silhouette approach, there was also a desire to keep away from cigarette card triviality." [15]

He said almost nothing about The Queen's head – merely noting that the designs were submitted without it. A sample repeat design was shown to indicate how the designs could be adapted. Detail was given about printing multiple designs in one sheet.

Beaumont reports that the Committee saw all the designs but did not consider those by Andrew Restall worthy of essaying. "It was then explained to the Committee that Gentleman had exceeded his brief." No comment is recorded, but they decided to choose three of Gentleman's designs "as second choice and that they should be returned to him for inclusion of The Queen's head." They ignored the idea of se-tenant stamps.

Essay featuring the Paul Nash painting

Clark then suggested a painting by Paul Nash might be suitable and another meeting was arranged two days later at the COID. This painting was later to be essayed and proposed as the Committee's first choice.

At 7.30 in the evening of that day, 9 March, Gentleman phoned Beaumont to say he was meeting the PMG at his home the next morning and could he have his remaining designs to take with him? This was agreed and Gentleman arrived at postal headquarters to collect them some time thereafter. [16]

The next morning he had breakfast with Benn who was seeing The Queen that day. Benn was enthralled with the designs and took them with him. His trip to the Palace is famously described in full, and with great gusto, in his diaries. [17]

He had prepared his speech carefully.

"What I wanted to do was to talk about stamp design policy generally. I said that the new Government saw stamps in an entirely new context as part of the arts and not just as adhesive money labels for postage purposes. That was why we had set up a Fellowship in Minuscule Design and wanted to improve design generally."

Fins and rudders of a Spitfire and a Heinkel 111 bomber.

9 March 1965. Six of David Gentleman's original designs for the Battle of Britain anniversary without The Queen's head and the legend GREAT BRITAIN.

Spitfire ditched in the sea with an R.A.F. rescue launch.

Wing tips of a Spitfire and a Messerschmidt 109 (used for one of the issued stamps with the addition of The Queen's head).

Silhouette of a
Hawker Hurricane
pilot.

Spitfire patrol
attacking a Dornier
217 bomber.

Spitfire attacking a
Junkers 87B Stuka
dive-bomber

A TIMELESS CLASSIC

Specifically, he wanted to have new definitives with "a more beautiful picture of the Queen on them". On commemoratives the criteria had been broadened and designers were keen to produce pictorial stamps – a most exciting field that had never been explored.

"'However', I said, 'this raised the whole question of the use of the head on the stamps.' The Queen frowned and smiled. I said that there was a view held by many designers that the necessity of depicting the head on the stamp was restrictive and embarrassing. For example, the Burns stamp would be difficult to put out as a two-head stamp."

It had been understood that The Queen herself had refused to consider stamps that did not embody the head.

"She of course was extremely anxious not to give the impression that she was the obstacle to new design. I said that I foresaw a controversy developing about the heads on stamps which I thought would be most undesirable. I said the pressure to review this particular aspect of our stamp design policy was growing and at the same time there would be great opposition to taking the head off the stamp unless it were done with royal consent and approval. In these circumstances it seemed to me that the right thing to do was for us to establish that designers could put in any designs they liked, that they could all be submitted to the Queen for approval, and that I should be able to say in answer to a question in the House of Commons that the Queen had approved a procedure under which all stamps of all kinds were submitted to her for consideration. This seemed to me to be the best way of tackling it and I hoped she agreed."

The Queen then indicated that she knew that in some Commonwealth countries the head had been removed or a crown substituted. Benn said that all he wanted was the right to submit stamps of all kinds to her. Then she said that she had never seen any of these stamps and would be interested.

"I said, 'Well, I've got some in my bag' (having brought David Gentleman's collection

as provided this morning). The Queen wanted me to leave the new designs with her but I explained the difficulties and she agreed to see them on the spot.

This was exactly what I had hoped would happen so I unlocked my bag and spread out on the floor twelve huge design models of the stamps provided by Gentleman and also brought out his album of foreign stamps. I then knelt on the floor and one after the other passed up to the Queen the Battle of Britain stamps bearing the words 'Great Britain' and no royal head on them. It was a most hilarious scene because I had my papers all over the place and she was peering at something that had obviously never been shown to her or even thought about at the Palace before."

At the end he packed up and declared himself delighted to hear he could submit things to her for her consideration.

So Benn went back to the House of Commons "feeling absolutely on top of the world". He dictated a letter to confirm what had been agreed but had to clear it with the Prime Minister first. Apparently, Harold Wilson's only question was: "Did she get down on the floor with you?"

His letter to The Queen, dated 12 March, was addressed in deferential terms. [18] He was "delighted, and not at all surprised" to learn that there was no ban on submitting new ideas. He felt that the first step was to seek the views of designers themselves. New techniques and treatments could then be submitted to The Queen for consideration. He wanted to be able to announce this by a parliamentary answer in these terms:

"Her Majesty has graciously consented to consider for approval new designs, both traditional and non-traditional, for new definitive, commemorative and pictorial series. Designers will therefore, in future, be invited to submit any designs which they wish and these will go to the Stamp Advisory Committee for transmission for Her Majesty's consideration and approval in the normal way.

"Her Majesty has also consented to the use of a new profile photograph for use in the new definitive series".

A letter came back the same day from The Queen's private secretary, Sir Michael Adeane. At her "command" he was writing to say she was grateful to him for explaining the position.

"She has a considerable interest in this subject and certainly would not wish anyone to think that she is not prepared to consider new designs and ideas that may be suggested by the Stamp Advisory Committee and put forward by yourself from time to time." [19]

The Queen agreed to the terms of Benn's statement. However, there was a gentle, added warning which Benn was to misinterpret or ignore.

"She hopes that you – like [herself] – will keep an open mind as to whether her effigy should invariably appear on commemorative and pictorial stamps, in accordance with tradition, or whether it might be more appropriate in some cases to replace it by an emblem of Sovereignty such as the Crown or her own Cipher. This question can, no doubt, be considered when the album of new designs is ready for inspection." [20]

The next day, Saturday 13 March, David Gentleman and his wife Rosalind Dease came to tea with Benn. He told them about his audience with The Queen and Gentleman agreed to prepare a sample album of stamps, showing what could be done with different treatments of the head, royal ciphers, and crowns. Gentleman was naturally delighted with the way things had gone – "I just hope to God he is discreet." [21]

Thus ended a dramatic few days which had thrown British stamp design policy into turmoil. The number of stamp issues and designs had also caused chaos in the normally quiet Stamp Advisory Committee and they demanded a meeting with Benn, the same day as their next formal meeting (25 March). At this meeting Benn was careful to have minutes recorded on his side.

Members of the COID were met by Benn with sympathy. When they protested about the number of issues and late decisions Benn agreed that next year's programme would be decided much earlier and asked the Committee for suggestions. He then gave them the news that The Queen had agreed to new definitives but this was not urgent. In the SAC version of this meeting there was mention of a possible walk-out but Benn clearly soothed their feelings.

Then he announced that The Queen had also agreed to consider non-traditional designs

"for example, pictorial series on regional landscapes, great houses, English Kings and Queens, and other similar subjects. These could be printed in blocks comprising differing designs of one denomination: the stamps to be sold as a block or singly. Such series need not incorporate the traditional Monarch's head. They might incorporate the Crown or the Royal Cypher, and/or possibly some other indication of the country of origin, e.g. the letters "U.K." He suggested that an album of examples to show the possibilities opened by this policy should be prepared and shown to The Queen. It was agreed that the Postmaster General should commission David Gentleman to produce such an album." [22]

A more lurid, and not entirely accurate, version was given by the SAC later:

"Other projects had then been discussed, in particular David Gentleman's idea that the GPO should publish whole sheets of stamps on one subject – birds, cars, etc. The PMG had put this idea to the Queen who had been delighted with it and had said that these stamps could be without her portrait. The letters UK were acceptable as indication of the country of origin. David Gentleman had been asked to prepare a number of sample sets to show to Her Majesty. Sir Kenneth said that he did not think the Committee need concern itself with the idea at this stage. When the plan was further advanced we should, no doubt, hear about it again." [23]

Gentleman's reference to "cigarette cards" when submitting the Battle of Britain designs was now used against him.

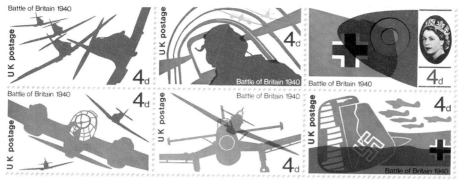

May 1965. Essays of a se-tenant block of six of Gentleman's designs with The Queen's head on only one stamp and UK postage on the others.

"The Postmaster General accepted that really good stamps take time. The 'cigarette card stamps' were by comparison easy, and a different kind of designer, chiefly an illustrator, could do them within a framework." 24

The fight over The Queen's head was to continue throughout 1965. On the one side were Benn and Gentleman; ranged against them were the SAC, postal officials and the Palace. In the first instance the clashes came over the Battle of Britain stamps. Gentleman prepared the artwork for the three chosen designs with The Queen's head included and these were then essayed. In his private conversations with Benn he continued to press for se-tenant blocks of designs. As a result, on 12 April, Benn instructed postal officials to prepare essays of six of Gentleman's designs as a block. One set was to be with The Queen's head on all of them; another was to have it only on the top right design.25

Benn saw these essays on a visit to the stamp printers, Harrisons, on 14 May and asked that they be shown to the SAC at their next meeting on 27 May. However, this was deliberately not done and the SAC recommended other designs. In late June Benn discovered to his surprise that the se-tenant block was not included in the submission to the Palace. Officials claimed that he had signed a minute saying the idea should be dropped. When Benn demanded to see this minute it turned out to be a lengthy paper into which a short phrase had been inserted, referring to the difficulty in producing multi-design stamps in the time available. [26]

Furious, Benn rewrote the letter to the Palace with new recommendations, reminding The Queen of her agreement in principle to the idea of unconventional designs. First choice was now the Gentleman block with The Queen's head on only one stamp; the alternative had The Queen's head on all. This was sent off but Benn almost immediately reconsidered. A phone call from his office on 1 July found Sir Michael Adeane, the Queen's Private Secretary, who was showing The Queen the designs at the time. He indicated that she was not happy approving designs without her effigy, at which point Benn made it clear that the Post Office would be happy to issue either se-tenant set, and left the choice to The Queen. She approved the set with her portrait included.

Thus, the Stamp Advisory Committee had been bypassed. Benn did not get his wish for stamps without the monarch's head, but he did succeed in having blocks of Gentleman's designs printed together. Controversy continued over the Battle of Britain issue when designs were released to the public. There was an outcry about the depiction of a swastika on a sinking plane, which made national news.

Members of the SAC were understandably unhappy at their treatment and the Chairman, Sir Kenneth Clark, resigned. In a very short letter to Benn he only cited the fact that he had been on such a committee for over 30 years under 13 Postmasters General. "This is too long a time for anyone to hold a post, however obscure," [27] but it was clear that he did not agree with present trends. Benn thanked him warmly for his long service and valuable advice, claiming it was a "sad blow". [28] Privately, he noted in his diary: "I must be careful that this does not get out to the press and be presented as a dispute over our current stamps." [29] It was stated by Sir John Wilson (Keeper of the Queen's philatelic collection and member of the SAC) that Clark had resigned because he would not recommend designs without The Queen's head. [30] Years later, responding to a question from Stuart Rose (Typographical Adviser to the PMG at the time, then the first Design Director at the Post Office), Clark wrote:

"I was perfectly sincere when I said that I resigned because I had held it long enough, but the words can be interpreted in various ways. There had been a change of outlook in the production of stamps with which I was not in sympathy. I cannot say if I was right or wrong but it was evident to me that there should be a Chairman with more liberal views. I was afraid that the admission of pictorial stamps would lead to complete banality, and I have been proved right." [31]

Commenting on Clark's views David Gentleman has said:

"Clark's judgement was that of a distinguished aesthetic autocrat who had been bypassed and sidelined. Of course there was an element of truth in his swipe: if a great many stamps are issued, some may possibly seem banal to some people. It's the selection committee's job to make sure that these are kept to a minimum – a task now complicated by marketing pressures, since stamps have to make a profit. But the alternative would have been to continue the essentially traditional, reverential and boring policy to which Clark had loyally committed himself." [32]

Stamps for Robert Burns

The bicentenary of the birth of Robert Burns had fallen in 1959 when stamp-issuing policy was still very conservative. As a result, despite much Scottish

lobbying, no stamps were issued. With the new policy there was renewed pressure for stamps and it was agreed that two would be issued in January 1966, even though there was no anniversary or event.

For this issue revised instructions to artists were sent out, clearly at Benn's instigation. Traditional design incorporating The Queen's head was now only one option. Artists

October 1965. "Non-traditional" essays of designs by Jock Kinnear (shown here) and A. B. Imrie for the Robert Burns stamp issue, without The Queen's head.

Essay of a design by
A. B. Imrie with the
Scottish crown.

Signature essays
with and without
The Queen's head
by Jock Kinnear

were also given "absolute freedom as to size, features of design, colour and art work" being encouraged to submit any designs they wished. Importantly, they were also given the option of omitting The Queen's head, to be replaced by the inclusion of the words UK POSTAGE, the Crown or Royal cypher. All artists chosen were Scottish. [33]

The result was a total of 40 designs of which 21 could be described as non-traditional – in other words minus The Queen's head. Most featured a portrait or silhouette of Burns but two bore his signature alone. One even had the cypher ER (*not* EIIR) and the Scottish crown. A large number of the designs were essayed and the Stamp Advisory Committee, now under the chairmanship of James Fitton, initially chose two of the non-traditional versions, those featuring Burns' signature. However, they asked that they be proofed with the addition of The Queen's head.

The issued stamps
by Gordon Huntly
with The Queen's
head

At their meeting of 20 October the Post Office representative informed them that it was very unlikely that any design without The Queen's head would be chosen, despite the freedom given in the "Instructions to Artists". [34] This was shortly after a letter had come from the prime minister's private secretary to the Postmaster General's private secretary (discussed later). So designs by Gordon Huntly featuring the two main portraits of Burns, after Alexander

Nasmyth and Archibald Skirving, together with the Wilding portrait of The Queen, were proposed as first choice, and approved.

The Gentleman Album

Back in March The Queen had agreed to the creation of an album of experimental designs with symbols other than her head but asking Benn to keep an open mind about whether her portrait should invariably appear. Benn promptly discussed this with David Gentleman and asked for his proposals. An undated list from Gentleman provided a myriad of ideas, from regional landscapes to transport, and plants and animals to the industrial revolution. [35] There were some 15 major headings and dozens of sub-divisions. Included were famous men and women (with Cromwell listed as a statesman) and a series of "Most-interesting-looking Sovereigns".

Much to Benn's officials' dismay there was no formal letter of commission and it took some time for one to be forthcoming. A draft was discussed with Gentleman and various aspects changed at his request. The final commission was dated 9 August. Listed were requirements for definitive and commemorative stamps and then the experimental designs.

"Pictorial Stamps: Sets of designs, three low values in each, are required on any typically British themes which allow the artist maximum scope for effective design. As with the commemorative topics mentioned above, the stamps need not be of standard size. If designed without The Queen's head the legend "U.K. Postage" and the value should be prominently shown." [36]

Gentleman had asked if he had to adhere to the standard size for his designs. As a result the commission was amended so that the question of size and format was left to him. [37] He subsequently created his designs in a new size, $1:\sqrt{2}$, and perforating tools had to be changed accordingly.

Work continued on the experimental designs over the summer but just before they were completed a letter arrived from the prime minister's private secretary, Derek Mitchell. It was written to the Postmaster General's private secretary after Mitchell had been to Balmoral with Harold Wilson at the beginning of October. He had taken the opportunity to discuss various matters with Sir Michael Adeane, The Queen's private secretary, and one of them was the Post Office and stamps. Adeane had said that he was "a little apprehensive in case the Postmaster General persisted with his ideas about postage stamps not bearing a portrait of the Sovereign". When Mitchell enquired if The Queen's views had changed since March Adeane replied:

"the fact was that The Queen had pretty strong views on this, not from any personal amour propre but because she was against a departure from long-standing tradition. In her relations with her Ministers it was proper for her to keep an open mind but there was no doubt at all that she would greatly prefer not to be faced with an unpalatable decision and one in which she might feel bound to reject the advice offered to her." [38]

When informed, Wilson apparently thought the PMG should not even commission experimental designs. Were they already being prepared they should not be shown to the press without The Queen's approval.

Benn was furious.

"It was an astonishing letter for any civil servant to have written for it contains within it a clear statement that the Queen might under some circumstances 'reject the advice of her Ministers'. This of course does not come directly from the Palace but Adeane had conveyed this impression to Mitchell and Mitchell had conveyed it to the Prime Minister, who has decided to frighten me off by conveying it to me.

There are many angles of this letter which require a great deal of thought. The first is that it looks as if my new stamp policy has been torpedoed. Whether or not the Queen cares personally about it, Adeane and all the flunkies at Buckingham Palace certainly do. Their whole position depends upon maintaining this type of claptrap." [39]

He pondered how best to respond, but in the end decided not to write to the Palace direct. His position had clearly weakened.

Immediately thereafter, he went to see David Gentleman and had first sight of the designs he had been producing with his wife Rosalind. Benn regarded them as "superb" but they also seemed to resolve the problem of The Queen's head.

Gillick cameo head & other symbols

When the first photographs were taken of The Queen by Dorothy Wilding in 1952 Wilding was briefed beforehand by both Post Office and Royal Mint officials. For coinage the resulting photographs were then shown to the Royal Mint Advisory Committee to help artists as the basis of their designs. Four artists had personal sittings, among them Cecil Thomas and Mrs Mary Gillick in May 1952. The effigy chosen for use on British coinage was one by Gillick, uncrowned and facing right. After her sitting with The Queen, Gillick exclaimed "I am now her devoted slave for ever!" [40]

1952. Original plaster cast by Mary Gillick for the first coinage of Queen Elizabeth II.

Looking for a new profile head in 1965 Gentleman now took Gillick's coinage head and reversed it so that it faced left into the envelope, as all monarchs' heads had done on stamps. The source was an actual coin rather than artwork or the original plaster cast. Gentleman had it photographed and then engraved a silhouette version of it $6^{1/2}$" deep, on a block of boxwood. Pulls (or proofs) were then taken from this block and reduced to the scale of the stamp design artwork. Changing the portrait from a three-quarter angle photograph to a flat cameo, and further formalising it by reducing it to a silhouette without any internal detail or modelling, enabled the head to take its place within a wide range of

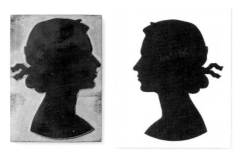

stamp designs more appropriately and effectively than the three-quarter angle Wilding photograph, which had inevitably been at odds with them. [41] Gentleman also created a variety of different sizes and shapes — solid within an oval or frame, and reversed out of a colour, again in ovals or frames. One could be placed at the top right of his experimental designs.

That weekend, on Sunday 24 October, Gentleman brought his finished designs to Benn at home. In discussion they came back to alternative symbols to represent the country, other than The Queen's head. Ideas included the E II R cipher, the crown or the royal coat of arms. [42] On the following Friday Gentleman returned with a variety of symbols including the royal coat of arms in various formats.

To little avail. Benn took the designs to show Harold Wilson, the prime minister, whose support would be crucial. Wilson had discussed the matter with The Queen at his latest audience.

"With regard to The Queen's head, he said that he had spoken to the Queen personally

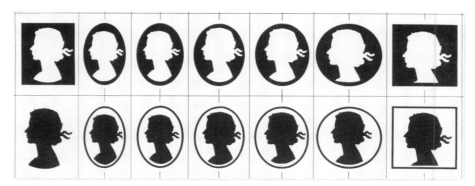

about it and that she didn't want her head removed from the stamps. 'She is a nice woman,' he said to me, 'and you absolutely charmed her into saying yes when she didn't really mean it.' He went on, 'I don't think you ought to go back and argue it out with her again because I'm sure you would win and she really wouldn't be happy.' …there was no argument and I told him that it would create no problems as I could put a head on every stamp and showed him the cameos. He relaxed and realised that this would present no political difficulties for him." 43

In practice this was the final decision though both Benn and Gentleman pressed on and when the album of experimental designs was eventually produced it contained alternative essays with the royal coat of arms in a variety of guises.

Benn now wrote to his officials to confirm the change of plan.

"I thought it would be helpful to report to you on my discussions with the Prime Minister about the new stamp policy and the attitude of the Queen to it.

You will recall that in March I had an Audience with the Queen as the result of which it was agreed that non-traditional designs could in future be submitted. The Queen's Private Secretary confirmed this in a letter dated March 12th and suggested that the Royal Cipher might be used on certain stamps in place of The Queen's head.

Following this the brief sent to designers was amended to take account of this decision, which had been announced in the House of Commons. As you know, a number of designs bearing different inscriptions and some with the Royal Cipher or a Crown were submitted.

Since then the Prime Minister has discussed the matter with the Queen. Arising from these discussions it has become plain that the Queen does now wish her head to appear on stamps, though she is content for this to be represented by silhouette.

It will therefore be necessary for the brief to designers to be amended accordingly and I should be grateful if you could let me have a copy of the current brief with a draft designed to take account of this change.

For the present no stamps should be shown at Press Conferences which do not contain the silhouette or portrait." [44]

This did not prevent an article by Fiona McCarthy appearing in *The Guardian* on 15 November entitled "Off with her head!", though none of the proposed designs was shown.

Album designs

Of the designs handed over to Benn in October 1965 there were 17 themes, including proposed definitives based on the Snowdon photographs. These themes had been refined from the original listing and now consisted of:

1 set of 16 definitives (on one sheet) using new cameo profile showing alternative colours

2 series of 18 rulers of the United Kingdom (on one sheet) showing possible colour sequence for one value block sheet

3 series of period costumes showing 4 examples for one value block sheet

4 series of famous men: 2 versions shown of John Dalton 1766 and his atomic theory

5 series of famous events: 2 versions shown of Newton's theory of gravitation 1666

6 series of butterflies: 1 example shown (and others on a separate sheet)

7 series of fungi (on one sheet) showing 4 examples

8 series of trees (shown as 4 examples)

9 series of birds: 4 examples shown (and others on a separate sheet)

10 series of bridges: 5 examples shown including Severn Bridge 1966

11 series of aeroplanes: 8 examples shown in different treatments of the subject

12 series of trains: 2 examples shown, and a set of 4 in a strip block of a complete train (and other examples on a separate sheet)

13 series of regional architecture

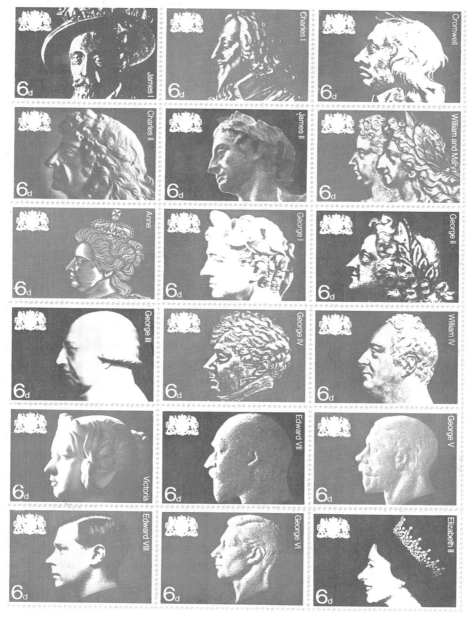

October 1965.
Artwork for designs
to make up the
David Gentleman
Album.

"Rulers of Great
Britain"

Gentleman Album
artwork
Seven Bridge

Isaac Newton

Puffin

Elm tree

A TIMELESS CLASSIC

14 series of regional landscapes: 8 examples shown (two from each region)

15 series of national coastlines: Operation Neptune 5 examples

16 series of famous events: Fire of London 1666 4 versions

17 series of nationally owned works of art (racehorses) [45]

The last had been added as a deliberate sop to The Queen knowing her great interest in horseracing, which had amused Wilson greatly when he was told. [46] Gentleman has described the task and how it took up most of his time for that year.

"Some of the designs were merely layout jobs reproducing existing originals like the beautiful drawings of nineteenth century ornithologists, or an engineer's drawing of a Victorian railway locomotive whose funnel I had to crop to get it on the stamp. Other designs I cut in letrafilm (planes) or engraved on wood (a butterfly, Old London Bridge) or photographed on site (the then half-built Severn Bridge) or painted in watercolour (British landscapes). For some of the Rulers of Britain sheet I used old coins which were deep bronze in colour; on these I used white poster paint sprayed on almost horizontally to emphasise the modelling; another Ruler (Queen Anne) I engraved on wood; for yet another (James II) I photographed his statue outside the National Gallery. Cromwell, a Ruler if not a Monarch, was simply a photograph of the famous coin portrait." [47]

It was decided to have one example from each series essayed (an expensive process) with the others presented as colour prints at stamp size. Each of the designs to be essayed should be with the Gillick cameo head in one version and the royal coat of arms in another. All designs were in the new, larger size.

This took some time. Towards the end of January 1966 the first essays were proofed but it was not until February that the new perforating tool required was available. Then all chosen designs were essayed and sent to Benn, Gentleman and the Post Office from Harrisons, the printers. Various types of royal coats of arms were tried out, and also in one instance a crown, but all designs were also essayed with the Gillick cameo. Gentleman explained:

"When it became clear that the Palace and Harold Wilson between them were unwilling to remove The Queen's head from any commemoratives, I simply replaced the proposed alternatives – Great Britain, UK, the Royal Arms – with a silhouette version of the royal profile then used on the coinage.

This was used in the Album and on issued commemoratives until Machin's specially commissioned modelled portrait was ready: I merely had to replace one set of film positive overlays with another and sellotape them down." [48]

News of some of this was given to the Stamp Advisory Committee by the printers at their meeting of 26 January. They had been kept in the dark about what Gentleman had been doing. It was only remarks by R. F. (George) York of Harrisons that informed them of what had been submitted to Benn. Because he had the artwork to produce essays York was able to say that "to his knowledge Gentleman was working on Castles, Costume and Old English Houses for next year and also on this year's landscape pictorials." [49] This was a misunderstanding of Gentleman's commission but it indicates just how discreet the commission was.

On 25 February Benn wrote to The Queen's private secretary saying that the album of experimental designs was now ready.

"These are, of course, all samples and there is no question of the Post Office committing itself to accepting any of them for issue as stamps. They have been prepared solely to show what could be done and to encourage a more intelligent and widespread interest in British postage stamps." [50]

Mention was also made of possible plans to show the designs at the national stamp exhibition Stampex in March which Benn was due to open. However, politics now put this on hold. A general election was called and such controversial proposals were postponed. It was not until 5 April that the album of designs was sent to The Queen with Benn emphasising their

Gentleman Album artwork:
Far left: Fly agaric toadstool

Left and below Stamp-size watercolours showing fungi

experimental nature but indicating that he would like to have a public seminar on stamp design at which these would be shown.

Martin Charteris, The Queen's Assistant Private Secretary, then took up the thorny subject of the experimental designs. He wrote to Benn a month later.

"I have had several telephone conversations with your Private Secretary about your letter to Adeane of 5th April and the album of experimental stamps which you sent with it. You will therefore know already that The Queen is quite agreeable to these experimental designs being made available for inspection by the Press and the Public.

You do not ask in your letter for The Queen's approval to any or all of these designs and it is of course understood that Her Majesty's agreement to their display does not imply her approval for their use as postage stamps. Her Majesty has none the less examined them with the greatest interest, particularly the use of the cameo silhouette on

Telford's projected London bridge 1801

2/6

many of the designs, and The Queen's preliminary view is that the cameo is perhaps too miniature to be significant as an indication that the stamps are British.

The use of the Royal Arms with the heads of past sovereigns has certainly produced some very interesting designs, but here again Her Majesty considers that very careful thought will have to be given to whether or not such designs are appropriate before they are adopted." 51

By this time the Landscapes pictorial stamps had just been issued, the first non-commemorative special issue. These had caused another row between Benn and the Stamp Advisory Committee and a remarkable number of designs had been essayed. Most importantly, Benn had insisted that the new Gillick cameo be tried out as well as the traditional Wilding portrait. Equally, that all Gentleman's larger regional landscapes designs intended for the album also be essayed and considered. In the end the accepted Landscape designs (by Leonard Rosoman) were the first stamps issued which showed the Gillick cameo and The Queen had already approved the designs without any comment on the silhouette. The cameo there had been rather larger than as used on Gentleman's experimental designs.

In the meantime, yet more problems arose with the use of the Gillick cameo. Postal officials realised that there might be a question of

Sussex · ENGLAND · 4d · L ROSOMAN · HARRISON AND SONS LTD

Harlech Castle · WALES · 1s.3d · L ROSOMAN · HARRISON AND SONS LTD

The Cairngorms · SCOTLAND · 1s.6d · L ROSOMAN · HARRISON AND SONS LTD

A TIMELESS CLASSIC

copyright and wrote to the Royal Mint to enquire, but only on 8 February. [52] An immediate response stated that the Mint *would* have objection to the use of the coinage head on postage stamps. This created a problem as work had reached an advanced stage. Benn wrote to James Callaghan, the Chancellor of the Exchequer and, as such, Master of the Mint. He told him about new designs of stamps but without specifically mentioning the problems.

Because of the election it was not until late March that Callaghan replied and the Mint commented. The Deputy Master wrote to the Treasury on 25 March giving a frank appraisal. He understood that a submission had already been made to The Queen incorporating a version of the coinage effigy and that this had been approved.

"Post Office officials are embarrassed by the whole business, and the Postmaster General's earlier submission had been made in spite of a minute recording the Mint's views. They remain diffident and uncertain.

I hesitate to take a powerful line without knowing that this would be endorsed. Equally, I hesitate to talk to the Palace because Palace officials presumably assume that any necessary clearance has been had and I would not wish to expose the position to them.

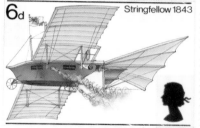

Gentleman Album artwork: Stringfellow plane of 1843

In the present case (as I said earlier) we might well recommend a relaxation but I do think in this peculiar sort of matter the least we can do is to try to maintain a proper procedure and that we should see that The Queen and her staff are not misled. There are obvious dangers in doing anything else." [53]

Benn decided to see Callaghan in April and a brief from the Mint was required so that Callaghan knew the details of the situation. The draft version was particularly strong.

"The Deputy Master's view is that, although there are precedents from earlier reigns, the use of the coinage effigy for any other purpose than coinage should be discouraged; it is not only the effigy of the United Kingdom coinage but also of other coinages of the Commonwealth. A rigid line is taken against all commercial users and the appearance of the effigy on postage stamps is an avoidable complication.

*Subject to your views and those of the Palace the Deputy Master suggests than an exception might continue to be made in the case of the present effigy. A new coinage effigy will appear on United Kingdom decimal coins and has already been adopted by some other members of the Commonwealth. He suggests that this effigy, which is the one by Arnold Machin approved by The Queen in 1964, **should be scrupulously reserved for coinage.**"* [54] [author's emphasis]

The final version was not so strongly worded but still included the interesting statement that the Machin effigy should not be used on stamps. It was not until 10 May that the meeting took place. Clearly, Callaghan gently rapped Benn's knuckles.

"… the Chancellor saw the Postmaster General yesterday on a number of subjects. One of these was the question of the coinage effigy and postage stamps. The Chancellor asked the Postmaster General to ensure that, in future, he approached the Master of the Mint [i.e. himself] before approaching the Palace. The Postmaster General appeared to accept this advice." [55]

That this was a storm in a teacup, and definitely a case of *amour propre*, is made clear by a previous request. In 1961 the Crown Agents wrote to the Mint requesting the use of the Gillick engraving on a stamp of St. Helena (a colonial territory for which they produced stamps). An immediate reply stated that there was no objection. With regard to copyright or a fee the Crown Agents should consult Mrs

The Gillick head on a St Helena stamp

Gillick who was living in the Kings Road. [56] The 3d stamp was issued the following December.

Over the same period in early 1966 as the argument over copyright the Stamp Advisory Committee also fought a continuing battle over the size of the Gillick coinage head. They tried to reject it for the World Cup stamps, especially designs by David Gentleman. Then they complained about its small size. But it had become standard.

Standardisation of design elements

From January there had been a new member of the Committee, F H K Henrion, a poster and exhibition designer. In March he drew up a memorandum on the theoretical and practical problems of pictorial stamps based on a view of Gentleman's experimental designs. [57] Henrion advocated the standardisation of design elements. He identified two major problems, one being the relation of what he described as "the obligatory

Gentleman Album: Essay of the racehorse painting design The Hero of 1847

informative elements – emblem, denomination and title" to the pictorial element. The other was the use of different designers within the same set.

As far as the relationship of "emblem" and pictorial image he found the flexible solution in the designs in the Gentleman Album. The "emblem" had to be one which

"A. can be clearly and successfully overprinted in a single printing, or reversed out in white, on a very wide range of colours, tonal strength and textures ...

B. is clearly recognisable at a final size of 5/16 inch high."

The only possibilities were a purely typographic treatment (the name of the country), "a very simple graphic device such as the royal cipher, crown or royal arms in silhouette", or a profile head in pure silhouette – in other words exactly what Gentleman had created.

This brief provoked a memo from Abram Games, a fellow member of the Committee and graphic designer. In particular he disagreed with the creation of a "house style" which is what he thought Henrion's proposals amounted to. He was against the use of an "emblem" as being undistinguished, lacking identification and meaningless abroad. This left only the Queen's portrait "since typographic treatment alone would be a surrender of a unique right of Great Britain which should be retained." Although Games agreed that the Wilding portrait was in every way unsuitable for stamps he was also critical of the Gillick silhouette. To the poor sighted it was unrecognisable as being of the Queen. Silhouettes of the size proposed were "a dangerous departure for stamps". He regarded it as a "ghost" emblem devoid of content and substance. Overall, he wanted freedom for designers and no restrictions imposed. [58]

Games's view was supported by other members of the Committee when they next met later in March. Subsequent remarks recorded that they generally

February 1966 Essays of selected designs from the Gentleman Album with some alternatives to The Queen's head.

Left Essays of Queen Anne woodcut design in two alternative colours

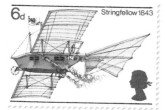
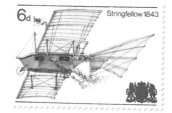

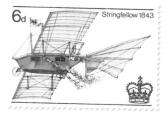

Above Essays of the Stringfellow plane design with cameo portrait, royal coat of arms and crown.

Left Essays of the Puffin design with the cameo portrait and the royal coat of arms

Left Essay of the Old London Bridge in 1594 design with the royal coat of arms

Gentleman Album Essays of the 1829 *Novelty* steam engine and carriages with royal coat of arms.

disliked the white silhouette but that "it could be considered fractionally better than its predecessor." [59]

Stamp Design Seminar

The "informal" seminar on stamp design took place on 23 June at Fleet Building in Farringdon St, London EC, home of the Telex Exchange. When Benn had informed The Queen about it he received an apparently enthusiastic, but carefully worded, reply (from Adeane).

"Her Majesty is interested to read about the seminar which is to be held this month and about 'The Sunday Times' Coloured Supplement, which is being published in July, and she hopes that the wide public interest in British stamp design which you have aroused in this country, and which is now being re-echoed in the United States of America, will continue to have fruitful results. You can rest assured that this is far from being a subject which Her Majesty regards in any way as 'routine'; she looks forward to the designs which you submit because she realizes, better than most people perhaps, that the postage stamp, which we invented, remains one of the best ways of reminding the world of what we are and what we are doing." [60]

Benn showed Gentleman's album to the Stamp Advisory Committee before the seminar. This was at a regular meeting on 15 June, towards the end of the period from which minutes seem to have survived.

"The Postmaster General stressed that the surface had so far only been scratched and that there were many other possibilities – stamps on Road Safety or Public Health, for

Trees in Britain

Watercolour drawings of native trees,
as they appear at different seasons

Pages from the
David Gentleman
Album showing
essays and stamp-
size photographs of
designs on various
themes.

Trees in Britain with
the Gillick head

example. The page in the album showing stamps of British Monarchs suggested a very interesting issue." [61]

In his *Diaries* Benn records that then the criticism began. [62] Once again the phrase "cigarette cards" was used to describe some of the designs, this time by Abram Games. Others agreed. Benn then explained about the seminar where a quarter of the material to be shown would be from the Gentleman Album. The remainder would be accepted and unaccepted work by successful designers and some colonial issues where the Secretary of State for the Colonies had allowed the Royal crest or cypher to be used. From the archives came the proof sheet of the Penny Black with press criticism of that design at the time. Invited would be the design and art critics of newspapers and periodicals, and the philatelic press together with representatives of the stamp printers and a number of designers and of course all SAC members. Benn would take the chair.

"Mr Fitton stressed that it could be embarrassing to Committee members to have to give an opinion, for example, on the Gentleman album, as it was generally felt that in having laid down his own brief, Mr Gentleman had side-stepped the real problem of British stamp design, the integration of the Queen's portrait with subject matter." [63]

It was agreed that the press would be asked not to attribute opinions to individuals or the Committee as a whole.

At the seminar a week later there were 12 frames of the Gentleman Album essays and original artwork. The successful and unsuccessful designs for the British Birds stamps, to be previewed that afternoon, were also on show as were the stamps and essays previously mentioned, and a selection of children's paintings submitted for the Christmas issue. A memorandum was provided giving a précis of what had happened in British stamp design over the preceding two years. This, of course, was almost the first indication the public had of what had been happening behind the scenes.

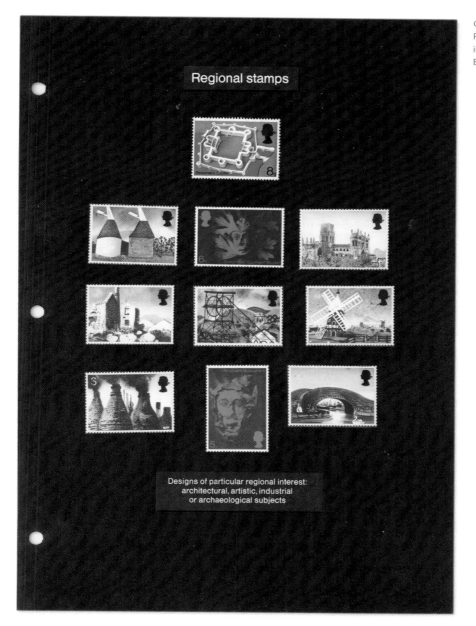

Regional stamps

Designs of particular regional interest:
architectural, artistic, industrial
or archaeological subjects

Benn took the chair and it was well attended by artists, philatelic journalists and members of the Stamp Advisory Committee. In the discussion which took place opinion was divided about whether too many stamps were being issued. When it came to The Queen's head stamp designers were always "disturbed" about the problem of integrating it into the design. Minutes record that:

"The Head must retain an element of permanency, a classic, ageless quality; yet every artist had his own way of working and there must therefore be a number of Heads from which he could choose or one basic Head from which a number of treatments could emerge. Whatever emerged must be easily recognisable and must not raise the same problems of integration as the Head." [64]

There could be a classic design for definitives and an easily recognisable symbol or emblem for commemoratives. Then there was the problem of the U.P.U. stipulation that postage stamps must bear an indication of country of origin.

"The introduction of a variety of symbols/ciphers/Heads might lead to our being challenged on the fact that we were not conforming to U.P.U. Regulations." [65]

In his *Diaries* Benn recorded that Fitton "intervened regularly and rather violently" [66] As Chairman of the SAC he felt on the defensive, Benn thought.

"I am sure that the seminar justified itself up to the hilt in that the discussion from now on will be intelligent and informed." [67]

Later that afternoon at the press conference for the Birds stamps he was challenged directly as to whether he would take The Queen's head off stamps. He replied:

"'I cannot visualise the time …' This was deliberately ambiguous and will not prevent us from submitting the Rulers of Great Britain series to the Palace for next February. I felt I was marginally betraying my cause, but things have to change slowly." [68]

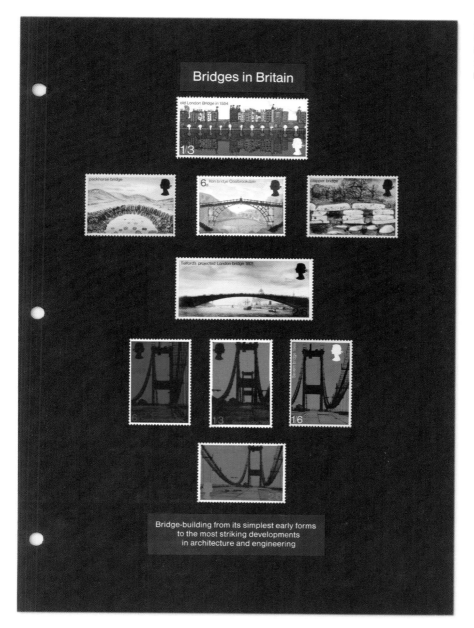

Gentleman Album:
Bridges in Britain
including the
Severn Bridge
being built

On 1 July Benn wrote to The Queen to inform her of the success of his seminar mentioning the favourable comments and specifically ideas for the 1967 programme. Adeane's reply on the 4th referred to this:

"You mention specifically your 1967 programme and the 'Rulers of Great Britain' series from the Gentleman Album. The Queen has, of course, seen this already and we sent it back to Post Office Headquarters, but she would very much like to have another look at the block before considering the problem of whether the Royal Crest or the Gold profile should be used to identify these stamps. Could you very kindly have it sent round for Her Majesty to inspect again?" [69]

However, it was not to be necessary, as Adeane would certainly have known when he wrote the letter. In the meantime Benn had been promoted to the Cabinet as Minister of Technology and so ceased to be Postmaster General. As a result nothing further was to happen with the contentious Rulers issue, nor royal crests or ciphers. The new Postmaster General was Edward Short, someone much less likely to promote a revolutionary climate. When Wilson told Benn of his new appointment Benn only regretted that he should leave the Post Office at a critical moment and "on the eve of the announcement of historic changes." Wilson's replied that he had done an excellent job in modernising an old industry. "Now you must start learning and for six months you will have to keep your head down and read, and no gimmicks." Benn only commented (in his *Diaries*): "That from Harold!" [70]

So the revolution was over, with Benn sidelined. Nevertheless, the aftershocks of the ferment he had created in the Post Office continued to be felt long thereafter. This was particularly true in the world of postage stamps. Everything to do with them had changed – reasons for issue, the number of issues, subject matter and their design. In the end it resulted in the collapse of the system of an external Stamp Advisory Committee under the COID – replaced by the Post Office's own committee in February 1968.

Many new aspects of stamps were still in course of preparation or production (the first Christmas stamps with children's paintings for example), and some did not come about, as a result of Benn no longer being there to force things through (the proposed Rulers of Great Britain). However, a new definitive portrait had been commissioned and work was already in train. In the midst of the stamp design revolution the National Postal Museum had also been born, with the gift of Reginald Phillips' collection to the nation. This had been negotiated over the period by Ken Hind and was finalised by a trip by Benn to Brighton for the well-publicised hand-over.

Gentleman's Album was seminal. It introduced a new size of stamp, and themes and designs which were to influence stamp issues for almost 20 years. Many still look remarkably modern and very much as if they had in fact been issued. Themes such as bridges, ships, aircraft, buildings (both great and rural), literature, famous people, trees, trains, flowers, animals and many others, now became the norm in issued stamps, often with designs by David Gentleman. Many of Henrion's ideas of a "house style", based on the Album, also came to be adopted.

Stamps are a microcosm of the age, and reflect their country of origin. The 1960s was a period of remarkable social change in Britain. An era of deference was swept away and with it extremely old-fashioned attitudes to stamp-issuing policy. This was reflected in stamps as issued, and those proposed. All this formed the background to the work on definitives, and many aspects overlapped and intermingled.

Royal ciphers

Gentleman Album:
A selection of
essays showing
different forms of
the royal coat of
arms (not ciphers)

1   **Benn, Tony** *Out of the Wilderness – Diaries 1963-67 1987*, p14; also **Griffiths, Alan** *The Modernisation of British Stamp Design, 1964-1966* 1995 [BPMA unpublished]

2   ibid p179 (5 November 1964)

3   ibid p192 (24 November 1964)

4   *Philatelic Bulletin* Vol. I, No. 4 pp3-4, January 1964

5   POST 54/16 Papers, minutes and agenda of Stamp Advisory Committee meetings 1962-1966

6   Private communication from David Gentleman, September 2006

7   POST 122/12329 Commemorative stamp designs: David Gentleman suggests omission of Queen's head

8   Gentleman, September 2006

9   **Benn Diaries** op cit pp208/9 (24 January 1965)

10   **Benn Diaries** op cit p219 (15 February 1965)

11   POST 121/493 Postage stamps: design and selection procedure; composition of Postmaster General's Advisory Panel on stamp design

12   ibid

13   ibid

14   POST 122/9408 Postage Stamps. Special Issues. Battle of Britain: 25th anniversary of the Battle of Britain September 1965. Instructions to artists; also **Griffiths** op cit

15   ibid

16   ibid

17   **Benn Diaries** op cit pp230/3 (10 March 1965)

18   POST 122/10710 Postage Stamps. Stamp Design Policy: New look. Change to the Queen's profile portrait. Correspondence with the Palace.

19   ibid

20   ibid

21   **Benn Diaries** op cit p234 (13 March 1965)

22   POST 122/12338 Postage Stamps. Stamp Design Policy: New Look. Brief for experimental designs by David Gentleman

23   POST 122/10737 Postage Stamps. Special Stamp Issues. 1965 Programme: Sir Winston Churchill.

24   ibid

25   POST 122/9410 Postage Stamps. Special Issues. Battle of Britain: PMG's instructions for the production of the 'block of six essays'.

26 **Benn Diaries** op cit pp281/2 (29 June 1965); also **Griffiths** op cit

27 POST 121/493 Postage stamps: design and selection procedure; composition of Postmaster General's Advisory Panel on stamp design

28 ibid

29 **Benn Diaries** op cit p332 (5 October 1965)

30 POST 54/16 op cit (meeting of 20 October 1965)

31 **Rose, Stuart** *Royal Mail Stamps a survey of British stamp design* 1980 pp59/62

32 Gentleman, September 2006

33 POST 122/10640 Postage Stamps. Special Issues. 1966. Robert Burns: Special commemorative stamp. Instructions to artists; **Griffiths** op cit; BPMA stamp history Robert Burns

34 POST 54/16 op cit

35 POST 122/12338 op cit

36 POST 122/12339 Postage Stamps: Experimental Designs. PMG's Brief to David Gentleman

37 ibid

38 POST 122/12341 Postage Stamps: Queen's portrait: correspondence Prime Minister/PMG; also POST 122/9851 Postage Stamps. Correspondence Prime Minister and PMG

39 **Benn Diaries** op cit p335 (14 October 1965)

40 MINT 20/2258 – Queen Elizabeth II coinage: selected artists for obverse designs

41 Information from David Gentleman 26 June 2006.

42 **Benn Diaries** op cit pp338/9

43 **Benn Diaries** op cit pp343/4

44 POST 122/12341 op cit

45 POST 122/12340 Postage Stamps: David Gentleman – Album of experimental designs. Essays/photographs of subjects listed on 24 October 1965

46 **Benn Diaries** op cit p343

47 Gentleman, September 2006

48 ibid

49 POST 54/16 op cit

50 P57/72 Pictorial Special Stamp Issue (Landscapes)

50 POST 122/12343 Postage Stamps: Experimental Stamps. David Gentleman. Queen & Official Albums.

52 MINT 20/3399 – Use of coinage effigy on postage stamps; also POST 122/12328 Queen's Head, Coinage Version, for the PO side

53   ibid

54   ibid

55   ibid

56   MINT 20/2415 – Work for **Mrs M** Gillick coin designer

57   POST 54/16 op cit

58   ibid

59   ibid – meeting of 11 May 1966

60   POST 122/12467 Postmaster General's Seminar June 23rd 1966 – Fleet Building

61   POST 54/16 op cit

62   **Benn Diaries** op cit pp428/30 (15 June 1965)

63   POST 54/16 op cit

64   POST 122/12467 op cit

65   ibid

66   **Benn Diaries** op cit pp437/8 (23 June 1966)

67   ibid

68   ibid p438

69   POST 122/12467 op cit

70   **Benn Diaries** op cit pp440/1 (30 June 1966)

6

A NEW PORTRAIT

On 13 January 1965 Sir Kenneth Clark and Paul Reilly of the Council of Industrial Design visited the new Postmaster General for the first time, and at his invitation. Benn explained some of his ideas for new stamps in 1965 and how they might be implemented. Then Clark took the opportunity to raise the question of a new profile version of the Queen's head. He thought that one of Lord Snowdon's photographs produced for the coins might be best. As reported in later SAC minutes:

"Sir Kenneth Clark said that the Advisory Committee was strongly in favour of a new version of The Queen's Head. They wanted it to be in profile, and to be engraved from a photograph. He believed that there were a number of suitable photographs already available, and he thought that The Queen would raise no objection to the idea. At the Postmaster General's request, Sir Kenneth Clark agreed to provide a draft letter for the Postmaster General to send to the Palace asking for The Queen's reaction to this idea." [1]

Although Benn agreed he noted "It was a depressing but amusing interview." [2] As a result a letter was drafted for Benn to sign which he sent to Sir Michael Adeane on 15 February.

"Our Advisory Committee on stamp design, set up under the Council of Industrial Design, say that our stamps could be greatly improved if the Sovereign's head were in profile instead of three-quarter face. They point out that in the majority of stamps the objects represented are in a single plane; and to show the head in three-quarters introduces an element of depth which it is difficult to combine with the flat design of other parts of the stamp." [3]

Photographs by
Anthony Buckley
(of many)
submitted by the
Palace in early
1965.

What were The Queen's wishes and if there were no objection which photograph would she like used? A reply came immediately saying she had "no objection at all" to designs with her head in profile. Various photographs had been taken in 1962 by Anthony Buckley as a result of a request from Australia but they would be available for all. [4] Subsequently, more were taken in April 1965 and these were also made available.

When Benn wrote to The Queen in March about non-traditional designs he also added that he wanted to announce:

"Her Majesty has also consented to the use of a new profile photograph for use in the new definitive series". [5]

This was agreed and steps began to be taken to create new designs. On 3 March various existing profile photographs were sent to Harrisons the stamp printers. These were one taken by Dorothy Wilding in 1952 and two by Anthony Buckley dating from 1962. As requested by the Post Office Harrisons inserted these into an existing frame of the current definitives and produced essays which they sent to the Post Office on 15 March. At the time, essays of the 1965 Simon de Montfort Parliament issue had just been prepared by the printers. One of Buckley's portraits was also tried out in the new, long landscape high value designed by Professor Guyatt.

Full profile portrait by Dorothy Wilding from 1952.

At this time the fight was just beginning over David Gentleman's Battle of Britain designs without The Queen's head and the Stamp Advisory Committee were protesting about the sudden increase in the number of stamp issues. At their meeting with Benn to complain on 25 March he turned the conversation to the matter of definitives. He told them that The Queen had agreed to consider new designs for definitive stamps which would incorporate a profile photograph, and that a new photograph was being taken for this purpose.

"It was agreed that exceptionally about six artists should be asked to produce designs for the new definitive stamps. The Queen's head would be shown either as a photograph, or a drawing of a photograph, or embossed." 6

15 March 1965. Essays by Harrisons incorporating Wilding and Buckley photographs into existing frames.

However, it was not necessary for a new definitive design to be produced urgently and indeed not much happened with this until July (matters with radically new commemoratives being more pressing). On 14

One of the still photographs by Lord Snowdon, Christmas 1962 (see also pp 34-39)

July James Fitton went to see Benn at Clark's behest to say that he was dissatisfied with the photographs supplied by the Palace. He asked that special photographs be taken with stamps in mind. Benn agreed to write to Sir Michael Adeane to pass on this request. This resulted in the Queen's Assistant Private Secretary, Sir Martin Charteris visiting Benn in his office, an apparently unprecedented event, when it was suggested that Lord Snowdon take the photographs - though not before October.

In the meantime there had been a meeting of the Stamp Advisory Committee (21 July) when members had agreed that the Buckley photographs were "of very inferior quality" [7]. However, they were only shown two of about passport size by Fitton and so they clearly did not see the ranges of larger portraits which had been sent and which had been specifically taken for use on stamps. As a preliminary, it was decided that existing photographs and "the medallion portrait of Her Majesty for the decimal coinage" should be made available to the Committee. Reilly was to contact Lord Snowdon for existing photographs and to ask what part he might like to play in obtaining the new portrait. A co-ordinating role was envisaged. Clark's knowledge of the coin design process here clearly bore fruit.

The existing Snowdon photographs taken for the coin portrait were sent to the Post Office by Charteris from the Palace on 31 July together with the 16mm film Snowdon had taken at the same time where The Queen was shown turning slowly on a piano stool under several kinds of lighting. These were then viewed by the SAC on 11 August.

"The quantity and quality of these [photographs] convinced the Committee that for the first part of the exercise at least, no more photographs need be taken." [8]

It remained to find the right "artist-designer, sculptor or engraver" to produce a drawing. Although no further sittings would be necessary at this stage, after the artist had done his work "a sitting or two might help to perfect it." [9] Parallels with the coin design process are obvious. (A plaster cast of Machin's coin model was also supplied to the Post Office by the Royal Mint on 28 August.) Discussions about designers produced three names: Arnold Machin and Reginald Brill with John Ward as a possible third. The first two were to meet members of the Committee to discuss the problem. Machin was invited on 18 August being asked if "he would like to be one of several people to be commissioned to produce a drawing for Her Majesty's portrait on the new definitive postage stamp issue" [10] and although no details have been recorded about the meeting, results of their deliberations were reported by the middle of September.

Sir Kenneth Clark was about to resign his post as Chairman of the SAC. So he asked James Fitton to proceed with the search for a suitable rendering of The Queen's profile for definitives. Paul Reilly reported the results of Fitton's search on 13 September in a letter to the Deputy Director-General of the Post Office. [11] Five artists were proposed: Reginald Brill, Stuart Devlin DesRCA, David Gentleman ARCA, Arnold Machin, and John Ward FSIA, with a possible sixth - John Hutton. In the end, the last-named was not commissioned.

In discussions with the artists mentioned a preliminary fee was discussed, to be double the usual fee for a postage stamp, payments being separate "to the extent that an artist's portrait could be accepted but not his stamps." Reilly continued:

"It seems that there are two chief possibilities. First, the execution of a bas relief portrait which could be used to provide alternative heads for designers' use, according to the lighting under which it is photographed and from which an engraving could also be made. Secondly, a drawn head, which would be reproduced facsimile, thus affording only one version; alternative versions would have to be from alternative drawings." [12]

A draft brief was attached. They were in touch with regard to the provision of prints of Snowdon's photographs. All the proposed artists had already been contacted and had provided their photographic requirements. These were attached to Reilly's letter. They were sent either direct or via the COID on 8 October. These dates indicate that all the artists had already agreed to take on the work even though the formal commissioning and instructions were not sent out until the end of November. One artist, at least, did not wait for this.

Initial Designs by David Gentleman for a Permanent Series

David Gentleman received the Snowdon photographs direct from the Post Office at a time when he was working on his album of experimental designs, complete with the adapted Gillick cameo head. Benn first saw these on Wednesday, 20 October and the discussion must have turned to the new definitives. By the following Sunday Gentleman had "added a complete set of definitives along the lines of the suggestion I had made of a white silhouette on backgrounds of different colours." [13] Benn thought they looked very effective and would prepare the public for the idea of a silhouette as the royal symbol on commemorative and pictorial stamps.

The designs in question utilised various Snowdon portraits facing left. Four were included in the final Album, with a variety of coloured backgrounds suggested. Other variants are also known. All are simple images based closely

October 1965.
Designs by David
Gentleman based
on the Snowdon
photographs.

on cropped images from the photographs with the addition of the legend "postage" and a value in sans type. It is not clear when, or if, these were submitted to the Post Office as part of the competition, but they were certainly produced before formal invitations were sent out.

Gentleman designs
based on Snowdon
photographs as
shown in the
Gentleman Album.

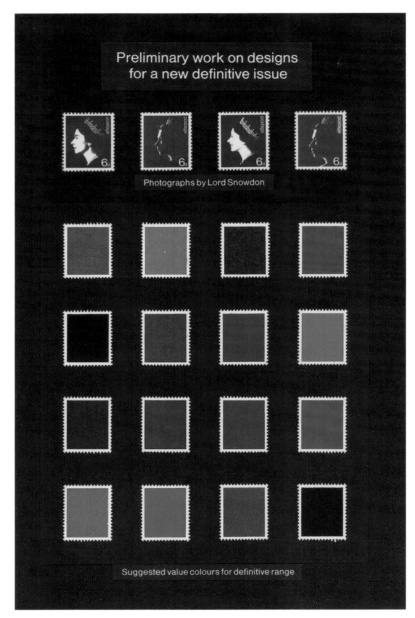

Preliminary work on designs
for a new definitive issue

Photographs by Lord Snowdon

Suggested value colours for definitive range

A TIMELESS CLASSIC

Instructions to Artists

A draft brief for artists was created by the COID and sent with Reilly's letter. Benn asked to see it before it was sent out and then made a number of amendments. He enquired about the requirement to include the words "Postage" and "Revenue". Advice from his officials indicated that the inclusion of "Postage" was the result of a *recommendation* at the UPU Congress of 1934 and so was not obligatory.

"The reason for including REVENUE *is that the low value stamps may be used for revenue purposes, e.g. on receipts; and the Inland Revenue Department have said in the past that if* POSTAGE *is shown in the design* REVENUE *should also appear, but that they would have no objection to the omission of both words."* [14]

Officials therefore recommended that artists should be asked to submit designs with and without both words "so that we can judge the case on artistic merit". Benn annotated this memo with glee:

"This is encouraging news. Thank you. I agree wholeheartedly." [15]

He then made various amendments to the draft to allow the use of a different profile head on commemoratives and definitives, and the omission of the words "Postage" and "Revenue".

The amended Instructions were sent out with formal invitations to the five artists on 29 November 1965. Two items were required: a rendering for the new portrait, and designs for definitive stamps using the profile portrait. The new portrait should be a profile and conceived expressly for the purpose of postage stamps, printed both in gravure and line-engraved (for low and high values respectively).

*"The head should lend itself to **possible** incorporation with graphic work; this is especially necessary when it is used for commemorative issues which have double-sized*

stamps (specimen enclosed). Traditionally about two-thirds of a commemorative stamp design has been devoted to a subject or a symbol signifying an event or anniversary; the remaining third has been occupied by the Queen's portrait, the denomination, etc. **the new profile for special issues may not be the same one as is to be used for definitive stamps in the future."** [16] *[Benn's additions in bold]*

Although the profile head could be flat or modelled in relief "it would be advantageous if the artist designed his rendering in such a way that variants would be possible" such as a change in tone of the background or a change in lighting. Photographs by Lord Snowdon could be supplied.

For the stamp designs The Queen's head must be the dominant feature. The head should face left. Designs had to include the denomination in clear Arabic numerals not smaller than $^1/_2$" high.

"The words 'POSTAGE' and 'REVENUE' should also be included in at **least one of the designs submitted**. *The inclusion in the designs of any additional material, e.g. symbols, is left to the artist."* [17] *[Benn's amendment in bold]*

Artists might use one colour or two, "but in either case they should not use a background colour deeper than that of the current 3d. stamp." Details followed about requirements for the finished artwork. 60 guineas each were to be paid for up to two different portrait renderings, and again for up to two stamp designs. A further 190 guineas would be paid for each portrait subsequently used and again for each stamp design finally issued.

"Ownership of designs. All designs submitted and the copyright therein will become the absolute property of the Postmaster General. He will not make any alteration in any drawing submitted by an artist without the artist's permission. If any drawing submitted by an artist is rejected by the Postmaster General, the artist shall not make use of the drawing or design contained therein without the consent in writing of the Postmaster General, but that consent shall not be unreasonably withheld." [18]

> *"All designs submitted and the copyright therein will become the absolute property of the Postmaster General."* Instructions to artists

No mention was made of the Post Office using the designs for anything else. The covering letter stressed the need for close cooperation with the Post Office and the printer so that the final submissions would be suitable for printing.

Two of the artists chosen, Gentleman and Machin, are already well-known here. The others were Reginald Brill, Stuart Devlin and John Ward.

Reginald Brill (1902-1974)
Brill was a social realist and narrative painter. He won a scholarship to the Slade School of Fine Art. When he was 30 he became principal of the School of Art in Kingston-upon-Thames and within five years transformed it into one of the most respected art schools in England (now the faculty of Art and Design of Kingston University).

Stuart Devlin (1931-)
Devlin was a gold- and silversmith from Geelong, Australia. He studied at the Royal College of Art in London and then in the United States. After returning to Australia in 1962 he won a competition to design the reverses for the first decimal coinage for Australia two years later. (When this first appeared in 1966 the obverse bore the Machin head of The Queen, its use

predating that of the United Kingdom.) He moved to London in 1965 and later designed jewellery. He has since designed coins for 36 countries.

John Stanton Ward (1917-)

Ward was educated at the Hereford School of Arts and Crafts before going to the Royal College of Art. He worked for *Vogue* magazine before concentrating on portraiture (often royal) and book illustration. Elected to the Royal Academy in 1956 (ARA, becoming RA in 1966) he later served as a Trustee, and also as Vice-President of the Royal Society of Portrait Painters.

Designs Submitted

Portrait "renderings" and stamp designs were to be submitted by 17 January 1966 and all five artists invited agreed to do so. Any accompanying letters are no longer extant. However, there is a manuscript listing of what had been received by the Post Office which is not entirely accurate (but reproduced here as in the file [19]).

Artist's Name	Portraits	Stamps
Arnold Machin	1, 2, 3, 4, 5, 6	A, B, C, D, E, F, G, H, I, J, K, L, M, N, O, P, Q, R, S, T, U, V, W, X, Y, Z, AA, BB, CC, DD, EE
Reginald Brill*		A, B
Stuart Devlin	1, 2 (Plaster Casts)	A, B, C, D
David Gentleman	1, 2, 3	A, B
John Ward	1	A, B, C, D, E

* Brill was paid for two portraits and two stamps.

Each name had a symbol attached so that portraits and stamps could be identified.

Reginald Brill's "rendering" (although not listed above) came in the form of a plasticine relief model and two versions of a drawing. Two stamp designs were also supplied, the Queen's head in black and white on a coloured background - one in pink and one in blue – with different white overlays for value, ER and regional emblems.

January 1966. Two drawings of Reginald Brill's "rendering".

January 1966. Two stamp designs by Reginald Brill.

Stuart Devlin submitted two plaster casts of The Queen's head clearly derived from one of the Snowdon photographs. One had a large head cut just below the neck; the other was more distant and showed a corsage. He also supplied four stamp images. One was based directly on a Snowdon photograph and the other three used photographs of the close-up plaster cast against sunburst and bobbled backgrounds. In a darkish golden colour this gave a rather severe look to The Queen's head.

Unfortunately, it is not clear which designs were submitted by David Gentleman for the competition. None of the items in existence bears any

Left January 1966.
Artwork by Stuart
Devlin based on a
Snowdon
photograph.

Right January 1966.
Artwork by Stuart
Devlin based on his
plaster cast.

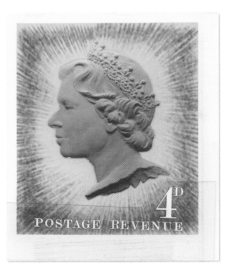

markings. It has already been established that he had prepared designs (white silhouettes on backgrounds of different colours) derived from the Snowdon photographs at the end of October. Four images exist in black and white and a further five different ones on dark, coloured grounds.

Also from Gentleman are photographs of pulls from slightly different wood engravings of The Queen's head. Stamp designs were produced from both of these images, some very similar in format to the previous photographic types. Others were much lighter in colour with different weights of font used in the legend, which could be either "postage" or "postage revenue", and the value. Eight designs have survived. Two others use a solid black silhouette of the engraving against a dark coloured background. None of these is dated or annotated.

January 1966. Portraits from wood engravings by David Gentleman.

January 1966. Some of the stamp designs by David Gentleman based on his wood engravings.

The "rendering" by John Ward is youthful and cut off at the neck. Five stamp designs are mounted together, with The Queen wearing either a tiara or the diadem. This is the only occasion where the diadem is known to be depicted on a design submitted at this time. When he came to send in his invoice some

months later Ward asked for payment for one profile portrait and one design, regarding the entire mount as one single item.

January 1966. Portrait "rendering" by John Ward.

Listed for Arnold Machin are a total of six portraits and some 31 stamp designs. In the 1969 GPO film *Picture to Post* Machin described, in retrospect, how he went about it.

January 1966. Stamp designs by John Ward including two featuring the diadem.

"I think it is generally accepted, at least by connoisseurs, that the Penny Black is probably the finest stamp ever designed and I decided to create the same kind of effect – that is with a light image on a dark background. … I decided to create a new design from a relief portrait."

"I think it is generally accepted, at least by connoisseurs, that the Penny Black is probably the finest stamp ever designed and I decided to create the same kind of effect – that is with a light image on a dark background. … I decided to create a new design from a relief portrait. I already had many studies which I had made when I designed the new decimal coinage. When I first began to design for the stamp I tended to use rather elaborate frames surrounding the portrait but gradually, by eliminating and eliminating, reached very much simpler statements." [20]

Certainly, several of the sketches hark back very strongly to the Penny Black. Others have elaborate frames, both portrait and landscape, and many give the appearance of a cameo reflecting the influence of Machin's work for Wedgwood. Some designs are repeated in different colours and a total of nearly 70 sketches exists, although Machin only mentions 52 in his memoirs [21] (probably not counting those still held by Royal Mail). There are three undated portraits presumably from this period. One is cut off at the neck, the other two have a corsage (one with, the other without, a tiara).

These profile portraits and the stamp designs created from them were considered at a meeting of the SAC on 26 January.

January 1966. Two portrait "renderings" by Arnold Machin.

"Mr Devlin's two plaques were ruled out as being a poor likeness although completely realistic. Mr Ward's drawings had not been taken far enough and did not show the promise to justify further work. The committee felt that as the portrait would have to last for twenty years or so, it must have some qualities of a symbol but that a bad likeness would be a great mistake. Several of the heads by Mr Brill, Mr Machin and Mr Gentleman suggested a possible treatment by blind embossing or by photography giving much the same effect." [22]

In terms of using such a profile head on pictorial stamps Fitton agreed to interview Machin, Brill and Gentleman together in three days' time to ask them to finalise one profile at least. There is no record if this meeting took place.

January 1966. Four
sketches by Machin
based on the Penny
Black.

A NEW PORTRAIT   127

Later, in June of that year, Devlin, Ward and Brill were paid for their commissioned work - £126 for John Ward, and £252 each for Stuart Devlin and Reginald Brill (plus minor expenses in the latter's case). David Gentleman was paid separately but as part of his overall work on the definitive head and his Album.

Fellowship of Minuscule Design

One of Tony Benn's ideas on stamp design when first he took up the post of Postmaster General was to establish a research Fellowship in Minuscule

Design at an appropriate institution. After various discussions with the COID and others it was decided that this should be at the Royal College of Art, tenable for two years. The brief was:

a *"to review the whole field of minuscule design with reference to postage and national saving stamps, and related matters*

b *to study the opportunities offered by modern symbolism and imagery for more effective recognition, communication, prestige and security in miniature design in this field*

c *to explore new techniques and materials, and*

d *to prepare a report including exemplary designs on which a national policy may be based."* [23]

This remit in many ways duplicated, or overlapped with, the work carried out by David Gentleman working directly to the PMG. It was also to provide a parallel route in the search for a new profile definitive.

In August 1965 Andrew Restall, already a successful stamp designer of the 1964 Forth Road Bridge stamps, one of the forthcoming Battle of Britain stamps and the 1965 International Telecommunications Union set, was awarded the fellowship. His work was to be controlled by Richard Guyatt, professor at the Royal College of Art and a member of the SAC.

Although there does not seem to have been any specific instruction Restall also took up the challenge of creating a new profile head of The Queen in the autumn of 1965. He worked with the printers Thomas De La Rue.

Bas-relief head of The Queen by Andrew Restall

Artwork by Andrew Restall based on his bas-relief.

white out denomination, Crown and 'Postage Revenue'
This bromide for position only — please use original for reproduction

This involved the use of their Geometric Lathe and Studio departments in the creation of two sculpted enlarged bas relief medallion heads of The Queen (without tiara or diadem). [24] Restall used photographs of these to produce some five designs, both portrait and landscape in format, which he showed

January/February 1966. Essays by Harrisons based on Restall's designs.

Ken Hind and Don Beaumont at the Post Office in early December. It was agreed that Harrisons should produce essays of these, though only four designs were used for this. The essays were ready in January and February 1966, just when the SAC were considering the initial results of the official competition.

In January it was merely noted by the SAC that Gentleman and Restall "seemed to be covering the same ground" but it had been agreed that Restall "should not be barred from participating" [25]. However, at no point is there any indication that Restall's work on definitive designs was shown to the SAC or in any way influenced the course of events.

January/February 1966. Essays by Harrisons based on Restall's designs.

When Benn wrote to The Queen's Private Secretary in February about the Gentleman Album of experimental designs he also mentioned Restall.

"In addition the Post Office has appointed Mr Andrew Restall to a Fellowship in Minuscule Design at the Royal College of Art and he has done some very interesting basic research on the shape, size, layout and typography of stamps as well as submitting very interesting ideas about the portrayal of the head using an engraving technique which resembles embossing." [26]

De La Rue later created experimental plates from their medallion heads, partly without financial authorisation, but by that time the main story had moved on.

1   POST 54/16 Papers, minutes and agenda of Stamp Advisory Committee meetings, 1962-1966

2   **Benn** Diaries op cit p203

3   POST 122/10706 Postage Stamps. Stamp Design Policy: New look. Change to the Queen's profile portrait. Approach to the Palace...

4   ibid

5   POST 122/10710 Postage Stamps. Stamp Design Policy: New look. Change to the Queen's profile portrait. Correspondence with the Palace.

6   POST 122/12338 op cit

7   POST 54/16 op cit

8   ibid

9   ibid

10   POST 122/10710 op cit

11   POST 122/10712 Postage Stamps. Stamp Design Policy: New look. Instructions to artists.

12   ibid

13   **Benn** Diaries op cit pp338-9

14   POST 122/10712 op cit

15   ibid

16   ibid

17   ibid

18   ibid

19   ibid

20   **Machin, Arnold** *Picture to Post* GPO film, 1969

21   **Machin, Arnold RA**, *Machin – Artist of an Icon* p136

22   POST 54/16 op cit

23   POST 122/10058 Postage Stamp Design. Fellowship in Minuscule Design: Agreement to establish a Research Fellowship in Stamp Design at Royal College of Art.

24   POST 122/10065 Postage Stamp Design. Fellowship in Minuscule Design: Thomas De La Rue accounts for experimental work.

7

FROM COIN TO STAMP

After the first consideration by the SAC of the various designs submitted by the five artists, James Fitton contacted both Machin and Brill (and possibly David Gentleman) and discussed their designs with them. No notes exist as to these conversations, nor for most of what happened during 1966. Very little documentation seems to have been created so the story has to be reconstructed from the evidence of the artefacts which exist. The overall story is, however, relatively clear. Arnold Machin explained:

"Because I am a sculptor it was simple for me to work on the basis of a cameo rather like the early Wedgwoods. The model was first made in clay. Then it was moulded in plaster and this process makes it possible to refine the details by engraving into the mould before the final cast is taken. I do a lot of work both ways, both on the mould and the cast and if I am not satisfied I can remould and start the whole process again. It is interesting that my first heads were based on designs I had done for the coinage and the Penny Black was based on an engraving done in 1837 from the Wyon medal." [1]

Photograph of a rejected plaster mould for coins

This was Machin's very much simplified description of his approach to the creation of a plaster cast of The Queen's head. In reality it was a complex and long drawn-out process.

Photographs of the coin mould worked on by Machin. Remnants of the surround can still be seen.

Before he created his first clay model for stamps, Machin worked on reversed photographs of one of the rejected plaster casts for the decimal coinage. These had been prepared by photographers in Stoke and showed the head (and lettering) in reverse - meaning that the head now faced in the required left direction rather than right as for coins. The legend around the rim can be clearly seen in the first experiment. Thereafter, he proceeded to work on the photographs eliminating the lettering, drawing over the clay portrait and colouring the background, in various stages. Images retained the round, medallion contours. At least two had sketches of stamp frames surrounding the images at this stage, both with and without tiara.

Using his original sketches from life, the photograph of the clay coinage model and his drawings over the photographs, Machin then created his first clay model for the stamp effigy.

Creating a plaster cast

The process of creating a plaster relief begins with a flat plaster "bat" or base. On this a clay model (correct facing) is built up and moulded. To make the plaster mould a fence or frame is placed around the clay. Then the (plaster bat) background is soaped to form a release. Casting plaster is then poured over the clay. This sets quickly, giving out heat as it does.

Once set, the two sections part naturally. Often the clay is destroyed at this stage as some clay sticks to the bat, some to the cast. This operation has created the mould (wrong facing). The sculptor then plucks any remaining clay out of the mould by sticking lumps of clay to it, and thus cleans the plaster mould which is now a very true impression of the clay model. Minor additions to the relief can be made at this stage.

To create the relief sculpture the plaster mould is painted with soap and another plaster is cast. A little detail is lost but then you have the first impression of the relief in plaster (correct facing). One can remove plaster at this stage by working into it with abrasives or tools – in other words one can cut back. If one wants to add something then another mould needs to be taken and then the sculptor cuts into the mould – to be followed by another cast, and so on (as generally described by Machin above).

The first cast or "Coinage Head"

This first cast was created at some speed during February 1966. One reason for this may have been a suggestion from James Fitton. As has already been seen he and the rest of the SAC were strongly against the Gillick cameo proposed by David Gentleman for use on special issues. On 1 February Fitton suggested to Machin that a version of his definitive head

The original plaster mould for Machin's first head as it exists today.

might be used on commemorative and pictorial stamps.
An embossed head was one of the possibilities.

*"The first essential is of course that it should be as good a
likeness as possible, as any failure in this respect would
attract so much criticism that the merits or demerits of the
design would appear quite secondary. If we could get a head
to this stage of definition it could be photographed in a number
of ways and reduced and dropped into the roughs you have
already submitted for the definitive when necessary, but if approved it could be
immediately used for the commemoratives."* [2]

To meet the necessary timetable the head was required by the end of that
month. One initial rather rough plaster cast shows the full corsage closely
following the drawings on the coin mould photographs. [3] He then proceeded
to refine and simplify the corsage. On 3 March the SAC held another meeting
to consider progress to date.

*"Mr Machin's portrait had been modelled in clay, photographed, cast in Stoke [at
Wedgwoods], the cast sent to Mr York [at the printers Harrisons] (in an unworked
state due to shortage of time) and the photographs on the table were of the clay, and of
the plaster matrix (intaglio) variously lit."* [4]

SAC members commented that the mouth
drooped a little and made The Queen look
too solemn. "This seemed to be especially
true of the photograph of the clay which
nevertheless so far seemed to hold the most
promise." [5] Another comment was that the
neck was too long, but most members felt
that the modelling of it was good.

"It was however agreed that a photograph simulating an embossed treatment held great promise as one of the alternatives available to artists. Mr York was in agreement. He felt that actually to emboss the quantity of stamps in an issue would be an impossible task for a big run but was a possibility for one of the smaller denominations." [6]

It was agreed that Machin should proceed, though no more mention was made of its use in place of the Gillick head on pictorial stamps. No further work should be done on Brill's "as it lacked promise". [7] Precisely what work had been done in the interval by Brill was not specified. At this point, mention was also first made by F.H.K. Henrion of a possible photographic alternative (which is described later in Chapter 8).

Over the next month Machin reworked his models and photographed them under various lighting conditions. As so often he then drew amendments and highlights on some of the photographs, in particular of the plaster mould (the image facing right). Here he straightened the neck, gave the lips a slight smile, and rounded the nose a little. He then transferred these amendments to his model and did the same again, this time reducing the size of the ear and adding highlights to the hair, tiara and corsage. By now he had created a new, gentler portrait and a plaster cast was made (with the image once again facing left). For ease of reference this is termed Machin's "Coinage Head" (being directly derived from the head used on coins).

Again the cast needed to be photographed. It is likely that this happened at the printers in High Wycombe and a few prints exist lit differently, one with the cast stood on its head. Once a suitable photograph had been achieved it needed to be set into a frame and then printed at stamp size as essays. Although four designs are indicated by printers' invoices no artwork seems to have survived. However, there is a sketch by Machin which has a frame which may have been the source of the designs. It shows a central portrait

Photographs of the
first mould under
different lighting
conditions.

A TIMELESS CLASSIC

Left Photograph of the first plaster cast worked on by Machin.

Right Photograph of the first mould amended by Machin.

Left Photograph of the first mould amended by Machin.

Right Amended second mould.

Left Amended second mould under different lighting conditions.

Right Photograph of the finalised plaster cast used for the first essays. Termed the "Coinage Head".

surrounded by regional symbols and the value. Possibly, the printers created their own artwork based on this.

The head was used couped at the neck in designs 2, 3 and 4. Each of these had the legend POSTAGE REVENUE, a value and regional symbols – rose, thistle, daffodil and shamrock for the four nations making up the United Kingdom. The essays came with several variations of colour and background. Most were bicoloured, but a few of design 4 were monochrome. They were

Design 4

   Design 3

   Design 2

sent to postal headquarters by George York of Harrisons on 6 April. Rather hesitantly, he wrote in an accompanying letter to Don Beaumont:

"It is necessary to do all these variations in order to get a proper appreciation of the drawing. I think that we could by retouching improve the head considerably but at the same time, before going round again, I would prefer to wait for criticism from Mr Machin, James Fitton and yourself." [8]

Beaumont's boss, Ken Hind, forwarded the essays to George Downes, Director of Postal Services saying that the PMG would be interested to see them and drafting a note to accompany them. This gave Hind's trenchant and typically caustic view (with which Downes agreed):

"These are, of course, purely experimental essays. There is still a considerable amount of work to be done on the portrait before the Stamp Advisory Committee will consider

giving a final decision about it. My personal opinion is that the head is at present so unrecognisable as to be unacceptable but perhaps this will be rectified." [9]

From later correspondence it seems that Harrisons found their cameras not entirely suitable for three dimensional objects and another photographer was asked to supply photographs. [10] This was the John Vickers Studio who, under instructions from James Fitton, photographed Machin's plaster cast at the Royal Academy. A selected photograph was then used to produce further bi-coloured essays of design 4 in time for the SAC's next meeting in May.

A variety of essays was shown at the meeting, when Benn was present, but they did not meet with great praise. It was suggested that Machin cut the frame and lettering out of slate so that the whole design might be unified. The head had been "worked on" by Harrisons but "it was felt that the relief of the Machin work was too heavy, and that modifications would have to be made." [11]

"Mr Fitton asked Mr Guyatt who was the chief critic of Mr Machin's head to join him in meeting Mr Machin to discuss the next step. The Committee agreed that this work should be pursued so as to extract the ultimate possibilities from it." [12]

With these essays before them it was now agreed by the SAC that further photographs of The Queen should be taken with a view to possible alternative designs "from a straight reproduction of a photograph to the Machin three dimensional treatment." [13] Then the documents are silent, at least as far as Machin is concerned. He proceeded to work on his own with, or without, guidance from Fitton and Guyatt, with no reports to either the SAC or the Post Office, which became a cause of worry to the latter. By August Ken Hind was writing:

"Although we have tried on several occasions to find out precisely where we stand in the matter of new designs for definitive stamps and, with an eye to next year's programme, when we might reasonably expect finished designs to be available, Mr Fitton has been extremely vague despite the fact that he is in close touch with Arnold Machin, who has so far done most of the preparatory work." [14]

2 May 1966. Further essays of the regional symbols design with the Vickers photograph.

Plaster cast by
Machin of wording
and value for his
designs.

Simplification of the design

Apart from a short holiday it is clear,
from photographic evidence, that
Machin spent the summer refining
and clarifying his ideas for the whole
design, rather than the head alone.
Responding to the criticism of
Harrisons' lettering Machin produced
plaster casts of the wording thought
to be required (POSTAGE REVENUE)
together with a value (6d). At the
same time he experimented with
eliminating the various decorative
symbols. Glass artworks were created

from designs featuring the head in a cameo with value only, and with the
cameo omitted but the plaster cast lettering applied.

Otherwise, he worked as usual on photographs. Taking a photograph of the
"Coinage Head" plaster cast, he cut back the corsage so that only a long neck
remained. Using this as a basis he added hand-inscribed lettering for POSTAGE
REVENUE, gradually reducing this to POSTAGE and making it bolder. Then he

Glass artwork based
on the simplified
head and the
lettering plaster
cast

simplified it further by removing the wording
altogether but adding the 6d value from his
plaster cast of lettering. This was then essayed on
19 October (at the same time as the first
Hedgecoe photographs – see Chapter 8) with
simple, clear background colours of mauve,
turquoise, leaf green, indigo blue and cyclamen.
The colours would have been chosen in
collaboration with the printers.

Simplification of the design – photographic reworkings.

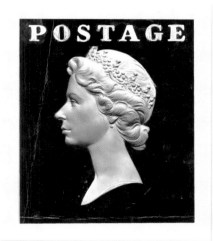 

"We had endless discussions about colour. The guiding principle was to find colours that wouldn't minimise the relief effect and blur the details. Colour without form, which seems to intrigue many people these days, in itself has no meaning for me. Patches of colours, areas of colour – all this I find extremely boring and elementary. Colours can be rich and give a sense of brightness without being garish." [15]

19 October 1966. Essays based on the simplified Coinage Head and value only, in single colours chosen in collaboration with the printers.

The essays were now ready to be seen by the Stamp Advisory Committee as the culmination of Machin's painstaking work over the year. However, in the meantime a photographic alternative had been prepared.

1   **Machin**, *Picture to Post* op cit

2   1 February 1966. letter from James Fitton to Machin

3   GPO Reg No. 1007B

4   POST 54/16 op cit

5   ibid

6   ibid

7   ibid

8   POST 122/10712 op cit

9   POST 122/10717 Postage Stamps. Stamp Design Policy: New look. The Machin Head. Preparation of preliminary essays.

10   POST 122/10712 op cit, letter from Paul Reilly to George Downes 19 August 1966

11   POST 54/16 op cit

12   ibid

13   ibid

14   POST 122/10712 op cit

15   **Machin**, *Picture to Post* op cit

8

A PHOTOGRAPHIC ALTERNATIVE

The question of new photographs to be taken especially for stamp designs is a recurrent one throughout this story. First came various images by Anthony Buckley which were not acceptable. Then, initial suggestions were satisfied by supply of the Snowdon photographs created for the design of decimal coinage. Yet the question came back, especially after the appointment of Andrew Restall to the Fellowship of Minuscule Design.

August 1966. Hedgecoe photograph on a dark background annotated by The Queen "No".

Immediately after the SAC's first view of Machin's initial plaster cast at the beginning of March 1966 FHK Henrion pressed the case for a photographic alternative. He said that David Gentleman was very keen on this, as was Andrew Restall, and it was agreed that he should find out in detail what they wanted. This came under the heading of the permanent series, but later it became unclear as to whether it was intended for definitives or pictorial stamps. At a subsequent meeting the same month (minutes betraying an element of partisan pique):

"Mr Henrion said that he, with Mr Gentleman and Mr Restall, were very keen to have new photographic sittings with stamps especially in view. Mr Fitton however felt that this should be left for the time being, until, in fact, a very clear brief could be

formulated. Both designers had previously declared themselves satisfied with the large number of Lord Snowdon's photographs from which they had been able to choose." [1]

When Tony Benn came to the May meeting of the SAC (when Machin's first regional essays were shown) Henrion seized the opportunity to return to the attack. Yet again he pressed for a photographic sitting by The Queen and Benn offered to write to the Palace when the Committee let him know the name of a photographer. [2] An internal Post Office memo noted that the letter would have to be framed rather carefully to get round any implied rejection of the existing photographs by Lord Snowdon. [3]

In the letter dated 12 May Benn referred directly to the Snowdon photographs.

"These photographs have indeed proved most helpful and good deal of work has already been accomplished by artists working under the guidance of Mr James Fitton. A plaster cast of Her Majesty's head has been modelled from Lord Snowdon's photographs and experiments in lighting are now being made with it in an endeavour to achieve the ideal composition of a profile drawing for postage stamp purposes. As you will appreciate this kind of work inevitably results in a great deal of trial and error, though the artists were confident that they could in time attain the desired result with their experiments.

However, my Stamp Advisory Committee who, like us, are most anxious to produce a first-class portrait consider that at this stage it would be most expedient for comparison purposes if additional photographs of Her Majesty in profile could be made available to them. They do not think that the comparison they have in mind could be made without reference to photographs taken with the stamp designers' requirements as the primary objective." [4]

Sir Martin Charteris replied five days later saying that The Queen was quite prepared to have another photographic sitting and had provisionally set aside the afternoon of 22 June for the purpose. She did not wish to nominate any particular photographer.

"Unless there are very compelling reasons to the contrary, I think it would be greatly preferable for only one photographer to take the photographs. The Queen would not wish to sit more than once and I suspect two photographers at one sitting would be not unlike two women in one kitchen."

Sir Martin Charteris
17 JUNE 1966

"Unless there are very compelling reasons to the contrary, I think it would be greatly preferable for only one photographer to take the photographs. The Queen would not wish to sit more than once and I suspect two photographers at one sitting would be not unlike two women in one kitchen." [5]

The COID suggested John Hedgecoe as the photographer. He had been appointed to the Royal College of Art as head of the Photographic

Department, which it was intended would be enlarged and developed under him. This RCA connection was regarded as particularly helpful where Richard Guyatt was professor (and Andrew Restall had his fellowship) and Guyatt would accompany Hedgecoe to the Palace for a preliminary visit when he could brief the photographer as to requirements. One suggestion was that The Queen might be photographed with and without a tiara for "commemorative postage stamps". [6] This is the first recorded mention of the possible use of these photographs for any other purpose than definitives.

After the sitting Hedgecoe informed the Palace that he was very pleased with the results and Charteris wrote to say that The Queen would wish to see them before any decision is made on which are to be used. At this point Tony Benn was replaced by Edward Short as Postmaster General and so it was the latter who sent the prints to Balmoral on 12 August.

"As explained in the earlier correspondence the purpose of the photographs is to assist in producing a composite profile. However this does not preclude the use of a particular photograph itself as the profile and I should be grateful if you would let me know which of the photographs Her Majesty considers suitable for use in this way.

We have it in mind to use the profile on the new definitive stamps which I hope to issue next year. It, or a variant of it, will also be used in next year's special issues." [7]

August 1966.
Hedgecoe
photographs – dark
and light profiles
emphatically
annotated by The
Queen "NO

The special issues would not include the pictorial series depicting the "Rulers of Great Britain" from David Gentleman's Album, something which The Queen had "noted" when Charteris replied.

Hedgecoe Photographs

Hedgecoe invoiced the Post Office for 60 photographs without differentiating between sizes or duplication. As sent to the Post Office, and thence to The Queen, they came in two formats. All were mounted on board, some at stamp size (three examples the same on each board), others much larger approximately 9" x 11". They showed The Queen wearing a tiara, but not that previously used, or the diadem as on the Wilding photograph (and the Penny Black). None submitted depicted her without, as previously suggested. All showed a true profile facing left, some in very dark shadow or silhouette. The photographs were returned from The Queen at Balmoral on 14 August with comments.

September 1966. Hedgecoe photograph sent to the printers Harrisons and the basis for the first essays.

"The Queen has looked through these with great interest and I am glad to say that they are generally acceptable to Her Majesty.

The Queen particularly likes one of the dark silhouette profiles, and as you will see has written 'good' below it.

Her Majesty has also written 'yes' against certain of the photographs and 'no' against others, and I hope that these written comments of The Queen's will give you an adequate indication of Her Majesty's wishes in regard to these photographs." [8]

Comments by The Queen were often quite emphatic (NO) though it is not always immediately obvious as to what she found objectionable.

Confusion as to their intended use continued. When Paul Reilly of the COID wrote to the Post Office on 19 August defending Fitton and Machin and their apparent lack of progress he also explained the reasoning behind the Hedgecoe photographs.

"Mr Hedg[e]coe's photographs were undertaken at the instance of Mr Henrion, who felt that a photographic solution should be put in hand, so that designers of future pictorials might have alternative heads to choose from. It has never, as far as we know, been considered that Mr Hedg[e]coe's photographic portraits should be used in the permanent series." [9]

19 October 1966. Essays by Harrisons based directly on the Hedgecoe photograph.

Nevertheless, they were considered. There seems to be very little documentary evidence as to what now happened with the approved

November 1966.
Artwork by David
Gentleman based
on Hedgecoe
photographs.

(viii) single colour version — in any colours
in range A or B.

(ix) two-colour version — as above, but
type and denomination in <u>black</u> on
solid colour.

photographs, as minutes for Stamp Advisory Committee meetings of the period are missing or non-existent. Two photographs were sent direct to the printers Harrisons by James Fitton in September. [10] Essays in blue-black and purple were produced directly from one of these Hedgecoe photographs on 19 October with the addition of the denomination 6d from the plaster cast sculpted by Machin. They were not regarded as very good but George York felt that they could be improved.

Thus, it may have been Harrisons who commissioned David Gentleman for he subsequently produced eight pieces of artwork based on two photographs, one a dark silhouette. In both The Queen is wearing the diadem. These were sent to the printers and essays were created from them in a variety of colours suggested by Gentleman, though not before 7 December

December 1966.
Essays of the
Gentleman designs
with a white
background.

by which point Machin's final design had been developed. Harrisons still persisted, however, with more essays produced on 20 December. By this time it was clear to all that Machin's improved design was much superior to any transient photograph, no matter how good.

1   POST 54/16 op cit

2   ibid

3   POST 122/10718 Postage Stamps. Stamp Design Policy: New look. Arrangements for John Hedgecoe…

4   ibid

5   ibid

6   ibid

7   ibid

8   ibid

9   POST 122/10712 op cit

10 P52/71 Special stamps 1967. Memo by Ken Hind.

TIMELESS AND CLASSIC

When James Fitton met the new Postmaster General, Edward Short, on 29 September 1966 he brought along the latest work on the new definitives. He said that work on the bas-relief by Machin was almost complete and showed him a photograph. However, he wanted "some fresh work done on it" and thought "there should be a variant showing the Queen wearing a crown." [1] All this work should be finished within six weeks.

Edward Short, new Postmaster General, official photograph, 1966.

Machin's sculpture at this time still included the tiara and derived ultimately from his work on coins and the Snowdon photographs. From Fitton's comments it seems that he had already talked to Machin about replacing this tiara with a "crown", more correctly the diadem (sometimes described as a coronet) as worn in most of the Hedgecoe photographs. It would be reasonable to infer that Machin's simplified "Coinage" essays had been compared with the contemporary direct Hedgecoe photograph essays, with the style of the former preferred, but with the diadem rather than the tiara.

The Diadem

A diadem is a completely circular head ornament. This famous and beautiful example was made by Rundell, Bridge & Rundell, silversmiths to the King, in 1820 for the coronation of King George IV. It is set with 1,333 diamonds

The diadem created
in 1820 for the
coronation of King
George IV.

with a pearl base, having the national emblems of the rose, thistle and
shamrock alternating with crosses patée. Although regularly worn by queens
regnant and consort from Queen Adelaide onwards it was originally designed
for King George IV to be worn outside a velvet Cap of State. It appears worn
by Queen Victoria (without the Cap) on the Penny Black and all of her
subsequent stamps. The Wilding definitives also showed Queen Elizabeth
wearing it, the photograph having been taken before her coronation. Today
the diadem is worn by The Queen when travelling to and from the State
Opening of Parliament.

The "Diadem Head"

There is no documentation as to what Machin did over the four weeks in
October but it is now that a remarkable transformation took place in his
sculpture. One of Machin's sketches supposedly done at the time of his work
on coins features The Queen wearing the diadem but without a necklace. A
photograph of the diadem was also supplied to him at that time. However, it
is much more likely that he now worked with one or more Hedgecoe

photographs as additional source material. This may be indicated by the addition of not only the diadem but also a necklace (as seen in Hedgecoe's sitting).

Other material by Machin incorporating the diadem also exists. One sketch features this within a laurel wreath cameo and this may have been created at about this time. Another

Arnold Machin working on the clay model.

drawing includes robes not seen on the Hedgecoe photographs, but this was probably based on a profile Wilding photograph. However, none of these are dated and cannot be definitely stated to have come from this period. Generally speaking, it is often the case that an artist responds immediately to some new stimulus and this may well be what happened here (the new stimulus being the request for a "coronet", with the Hedgecoe photographs as a source).

From new clay model, through mould to plaster cast, the same processes had to be followed as before. Again, the problems of lighting resulted in a large number of photographs of the finished cast. In some of these the background of the cast has been blackened in order to make the head stand out more in relief. This process was complete by 25 October when bromides of the new "Diadem Head" were sent to

The original plaster mould for the Diadem Head as it exists today.

October 1966. Photographs of the Diadem Head plaster cast under different lighting conditions.

George York at Harrisons for essaying. Now there is an image which is recognisably close to Machin's final icon. But it was rather sharply cut at the shoulder and without any indication of clothing.

A Post Office note records a major argument at this point. Photographs of the new crowned sculpture were shown to the SAC who regarded them as "fundamentally right so far as artwork was concerned" but who wanted them to be handed over to the Minuscule Fellow, Andrew Restall, to be finalised.

October 1966. Accepted photograph of the Diadem Head.

"Machin was adamant that if this project were to go ahead he would withdraw his design. A compromise has been reached, SAC agreeing that Machin should proceed his own way." [2]

Harrisons essayed the new bromide in some of the same colours as Machin's previous tiara essays (mauve, cyclamen and indigo but substituted steel and pink for turquoise and leaf green) and these were ready on 31 October. They showed the head alone with no value, on

a solid background. When George York sent them to the Post Office he described them as "very nice" and "a big improvement over previous efforts." [3] They had been shown to Machin who had some "retouching of the sculpture" [4] to make but further essays would be available by the end of the month.

Edward Short saw them on a visit to Harrisons on 2 November and was immediately impressed. If the subsequent amended essays were good enough "he would want to put them to the Queen forthwith." [5] However it was agreed that he would see Fitton and Reilly before doing so.

31 October 1966. First Diadem Head essays without value.

The "Dressed Head"

Machin spent November creating a new sculpture, not just "retouching" the previous one. Up till now, it has been generally accepted that when The Queen saw the essays of the "Diadem Head" she preferred a corsage, and that from this preference evolved the final head. However, it is much more likely that she was later shown variants with and without a corsage and preferred the

November 1966. Stages of the addition of a corsage, worked on photographs of a Diadem Head essay.

latter. Whatever the stimulus, Machin's "retouching" entailed the creation of a corsage to eliminate the sharp cut effect at the shoulder.

To do this he photographed and enlarged a printed essay from 31 October, that with the "Diadem Head" but no value. If you examine the items you can easily see the printed gravure screen. As so often before, he then proceeded to draw on the photograph, adding a corsage in various stages and experimenting with wording at the same time. Three versions of this exist. From the last a new plaster cast was created in the final format. Since there was a considerable amount of addition to be made it is likely that Machin added clay to the "Diadem Head" plaster cast in relief and then created a new mould from that, from which a new relief cast was made. The new cast is described as the "Dressed Head" in official documents.

Original plaster mould for the Dressed Head as it exists today.

Now came the problem, already met, of lighting the cast so that a suitable

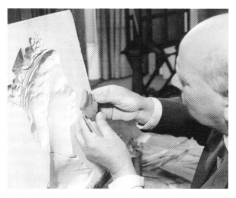

photograph could be taken. This took place at Harrisons, the printers. With the passage of time there is some controversy about what actually took place. In his memoirs, written late in life, Machin describes one occasion:

"All the equipment was first-rate, with the very best cameras of enormous size running on railway tracks, and with brilliant lights everywhere ready to be switched on and off during the process to produce an original Master photograph. However all this equipment, although most efficient in dealing with designs on a flat surface, was soon seen to be utterly wrong when dealing with any embossment such as my two bas-relief portraits in plaster. It was essential to obtain a Master photograph which would show up the relief in detail before the technicians began to work on the flat photographic image. After many trials and many rejections the final photograph was produced on a misty autumn morning outside the factory, using a mahogany Victorian camera and a photographer with a black sheet over his head!" [6]

This is the received version of the story, and it certainly took place. The camera still exists (Kodak Studio camera No.1, in the BPMA collection) and it was

November 1966. Photograph of the Dressed Head plaster cast.

November 1966. Artwork with light and dark backgrounds from a modified Diadem Head with rounded neckline.

6ᴰ

deliberately preserved as the camera used. However, some of the detail is contradicted by statements by the printers, also made long after the time. According to them "all sorts of artificial and natural lighting were tried and in the end it was done *inside* the factory [author's italics] using north daylight with just the right amount of cloud over the sun. This meant that each time the cast was photographed they had to wait for just the right conditions." 7

Both of these statements say that there was only one final photograph. However, this is clearly not true as more than one photograph of different plaster casts were used in the final stamps. Different casts can be distinguished depending on the background of the essay, either pastel or full, and therefore obviously different photographs must have been used, even if not recognised at the time. Certainly, a number of casts, apparently identical but probably with minute differences, existed at one time, and this would be consistent with Machin's method of working.

November 1966. Artwork with a dark background and couped neckline.

Essay Variants

From these new photographs essays were produced in differing formats, but normally including the sculptured 6d value used before. Delivery to the Post

Office was between 6 and 9 December. However, these were only part of a large range of essays created at the same time. Three other pieces of artwork were created photographically at the printers with variations on a rounded, couped neckline. These were essayed with gradated, pastel backgrounds and also with solid, dark backgrounds in a wide range of colours.

Thus, there were now three variations of head: the modified "Diadem" head with a rounded neckline; the same but couped; and the "Dressed" Diadem head with a corsage. Essays were with and without value, in one or two

6 – 9 December 1966. Essays of the modified Diadem Head with pastel and solid backgrounds.

6 – 9 December 1966. Essays of the couped Diadem Head with pastel and solid backgrounds, and with value.

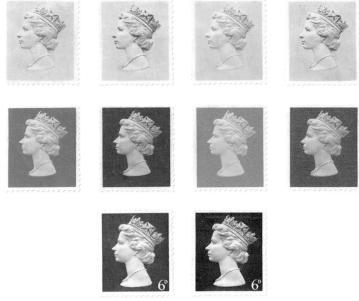

6 – 9 December 1966. Essays of the Dressed Head on pastel backgrounds.

A TIMELESS CLASSIC

6-9 December 1966. Essays of the Dressed Head on solid backgrounds, also with the legend POSTAGE.

6-9 December 1966. Bicoloured essays

colours, on pastel or solid backgrounds, and in the case of the "Dressed" head with or without the legend POSTAGE. Harrisons had also continued with essays of the photographic alternatives by David Gentleman but these were immediately dismissed when compared to the Machin sculpture.

At a meeting on 12 December between postal officials and the printers to discuss these everyone was pleased with the Machin alternatives now available. From the Post Office Ken Hind wrote to George York to confirm:

"I am delighted that the discussion we had today about the 'Machin' heads went so very well. It is a great relief to know that we now seem to be really achieving what we want.

This is merely to confirm what we decided at the meeting, namely for you to go ahead and provide us with the following essays:-

8   *essays in full background colours (including Stewart blue) with a specifically 'good' colour which we envisage using for a 9d. value.*

8   *essays in pastel shades.*

4   *essays in 2 colours.*

Half of the total essays to show the 'dressed' head, the remainder to show the 'larger' other head, i.e. without the corsage, varying these between the full and pastel colours." [8]

Other variants were to include the values 1s 6d and 1s 9d in the top right corner. The essays requested in December were sent on 6 January 1967.

"The colours have been selected with the co-operation of Mr Machin, and we believe that they are probably the best that are available, but subsequently we will send to you the full range of colours produced in the three heads that are shown." [9]

Referring to the "latest" head (i.e. the "Dressed" head with corsage) some were marked "A" and some "B".

"Mr Machin expresses a strong preference for those marked 'A', providing a small amount of retouching is done on the lower part of the Queen's face. As you will see, the definition of the hair and crown is considerably better than on those marked 'B'. I

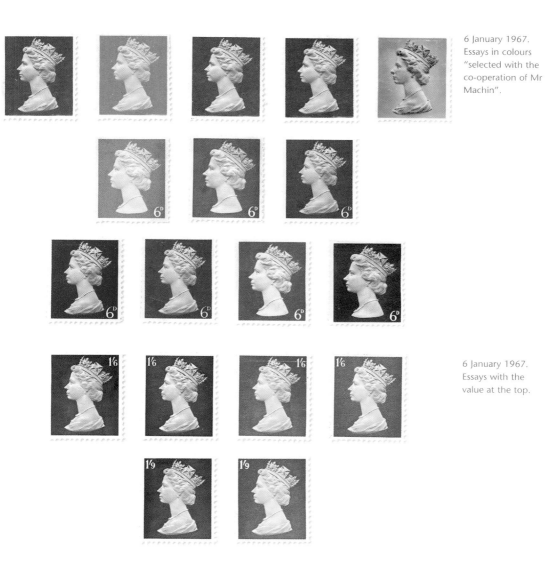

6 January 1967. Essays in colours "selected with the co-operation of Mr Machin".

6 January 1967. Essays with the value at the top.

agree with Mr Machin, and probably it is worth expressing this point of view to the Queen, so that if she agrees, then we can proceed further with this head, and this slight modification can be made before we go into production." [10]

The differences discussed here were the result of Harrisons' work on the photograph to produce a master image. Machin referred to the problem in his *Memoirs*:

"[the skilled artist's] technique was to work over every fraction of the photographic image with a very fine stipple, but I was concerned to find that the finished work obliterated any liveliness and spontaneity." [11]

The alternative left the photograph unworked and was essayed without value.

The Queen Approves

Experiments had been made with gold backgrounds, regarded as interesting (particularly by Machin) although they were not taken forward. A lot of time had been spent selecting the colours which, it was felt, were now "quite suitable" to send to The Queen for her approval. From these a selection was made and sent by the printers on 9 January for a presentation booklet. Included among 30 essays were examples of the "Dressed" head with and without value (and the value in different positions). There were also some of the "large" version couped at the neck. Names of colours were taken from the *British Colour Council Dictionary of Colours for Interior Decoration* (a standard work on colour published in 1949) and bore such names as Spectrum Violet, Russett Green, Medici Crimson, and some essays were in metallic colours.

These were shown to The Queen on 11 or 12 January by the Postmaster General. He reported back to his officials that "the Queen was very pleased with the definitive design; that she preferred the design with corsage; and that she would like the olive brown with sepia colouring for the 4d denomination." [12] Thus she chose the "Dressed" head at this meeting, preferring a corsage to a couped neckline. The colour which she "expressly requested" was a particular dark, solid colour for the basic inland letter rate (4d). [13] This was from an essay of the couped head – (No. 5 etch) in olive brown sepia, and was deliberately intended to imitate the original Penny Black - chosen for colour only and not design. Harrisons were instructed immediately afterwards on 13 January.

The first essays resulting from this (on 26 January) had the 4d value to the right of the head. This, however, did not leave a great deal of space for some of the other values. When the Stamp Advisory Committee saw the essay (at the end of January or beginning of February),

"they expressed their keen approval of the new design which they consider delightful and dignified, but suggested that the Queen's head be moved slightly right and the value inserted bottom left instead of bottom right." [14]

As a result essays were revised on 7 February with the 4d value now placed to the left of The Queen's head. Short sent both types to the Palace on 13 February saying that although he preferred the value to the left he would like to use both versions so that staff could distinguish better between denominations. Michael Adeane replied the next day saying The Queen "thinks that these have come out very well" and agreeing with the preference for the value on the left. However, "there would be no objection to using variant 'B' for one or two other values." [15]

One of the reasons for moving the value to the left was to accommodate the higher (larger) value symbols and this was noted when the original essays were sent.

"As you can see, we have now much more room to put in all values over 1/-d. At the same time, I am of the opinion that the readjustment to the position of the Queen's head has not detracted from the stamp in any way." [16]

12 January 1967. Essay in the olive brown sepia colour "expressly requested" by The Queen for the 4d value.

26 January 1967. First essay for the 4d stamp with the value to the right.

7 February 1967. Second 4d essay with the value to the left.

That was George York's opinion at Harrisons. It was not Machin's, who now wrote direct to the PMG.

"You will know, of course, that two different versions of the new definitive stamp have been produced. One which shows the portrait of the Queen in a central position with the denomination placed in the bottom right hand corner, and the other version showing the portrait off-centre and with the denomination placed in the bottom left hand corner.

I now understand that the latter version has been adopted for the new 4d. stamp, and I feel very uneasy about it because, in my opinion, the design is not as good as the original stamp which shows the portrait of the Queen in the central position. Apart from my own personal objection to it, I am sure that you will appreciate the difficulty that would arise should there be any criticism with regards to this particular point. Also, since I am not in agreement with the alteration, I would be unable to defend it." [17]

Ken Hind met Machin on 1 March to discuss the matter and come to some resolution. That The Queen had already seen and approved the revised version on 14 February made the situation delicate.

"Mr Machin's ground for complaint is that after he had spent months obtaining what he thought was the perfect combination of head, colour and denomination, the Post Office had overnight re-arranged the elements of his design and intended to present them to the world as the design for the next 4d. stamp in preference to his carefully worked-out design." [18]

Hind explained the reasons for having two variants (to distinguish different denominations) and that The Queen had preferred it when she saw it together with the original design. When Machin had been told by George York he had not objected "but when he saw a copy of the essay … he realised that the movement of the head was more than he had envisaged and it was this that gave rise to his complaint." [19]

As The Queen had approved the design in this form the Post Office were committed. However, if Machin would prepare a variant with the denomination remaining bottom left but the head better balanced they would be happy to consider it.

"After a very lengthy discussion Mr Machin eventually said that a movement of the head by what turned out to be on measurement one fiftieth of an inch, would meet his point." [20]

This would hardly call for a reference back to The Queen and indeed "it is doubtful whether it would be noticeable except to the artist's eye." It was confirmed that this would not upset the schedule and so it was implemented (being strangely, but consistently, described by Harrisons as 2/100ths of an inch).

Colours were now chosen for the full range of low value definitives (named as in the Colour Council Guide):

½d	Orange Rust
1d	Stewart Blue
2d	Horse Chestnut
3d	Spectrum Violet
4d	Olive Brown Sepia
5d	Oriental Gold
6d	Medici Crimson
7d	Paris Green
8d	Scarlet
9d	Winchester Green
10d	Olive Brown
1/-	Aconite Violet
1/6d	Tropical Turquoise/Garter Blue (2-colour)
1/9d	Tangerine Orange/Olive Brown (2-colour)

Before the stamps were printed the colours of the 1d and 5d values were transposed. Essays were produced on the L & M 7 proofing press in blocks of four

March – June 1967.
Blocks of four essays
of each value hand
printed in the final
colours (except the
1d and 5d).

A TIMELESS CLASSIC

for each of the values, from March through to June, and approved by The Queen on 29 April (3d, 9d, 1/-, 1/6d, 1/9d), and 26 August ($^{1}/_{2}$d, 1d, 2d, 5d, 6d, 7d, 8d and 10d). On the latter occasion it was noted that she was "glad to give her approval to these stamps which she considers admirable." [21]

This colour listing disguised variations within. The 7d, 8d and 9d value tablets were to the right of the head; all the others were to the left (with the head moved slightly as agreed with Machin, with the exception of the 1/6d and 1/9d where there was not enough room [22]). The 10d and 1/- values were on pastel gradated backgrounds; all the others had a solid or "full" colour background. However, different photographs (of slightly different plaster casts) were used with the different backgrounds. Philatelists distinguish them by noting a missing pearl in the necklace and two lines in the hair on those with a solid background; that used with the pastel background has a complete necklace and only one line in the hair. This proves that more than one plaster cast was made from the mould and at least two different photographs used as origination, despite Machin's own impression. Both had been used in essays from December onwards.

Bromides of the two different plaster casts on pastel and solid backgrounds.

With the higher values (1s 6d and 1s 9d) two colours were employed for both. Again the value was on the left "with the head remaining in the position recommended by the Stamp Advisory Committee" [23] There are no minutes of SAC meetings for this period and their comments are only reported by postal officials. The Committee was disbanded by Short in February 1967 just before these essays were created.

Paper

Until now stamps had always been printed on watermarked paper. However, postal officials felt that a better result could be achieved printing gravure on coated paper (where any watermark would no longer be seen, and therefore no longer be necessary). In September 1966 they asked for an experiment with the

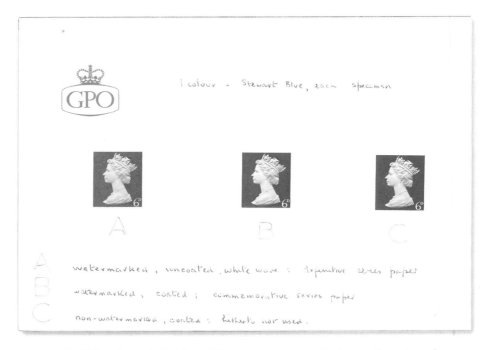

current (Wilding) 4d definitive. "The comparison will be useful when further consideration is given to the new definitive series to be issued next year." [24]

After the first essays of the new "Dressed" Machin head with corsage were printed in December an order was placed for essays on different papers. These paper trials took the 6d "Dressed" image and printed it in Stewart Blue on three different types of paper: watermarked, uncoated, white wove (the current definitive paper); watermarked, coated (the commemorative series paper); and non-watermarked, coated (Harrisons own paper, hitherto not used). The unwatermarked paper was Harrisons "ST 400" paper. They purchased the base paper from a paper maker and then coated and gummed it themselves. If the new design were to be printed on coated paper then it would be a useful point at which to discontinue watermarking. [25] This was to be implemented.

Gravure process

Harrisons held the contract for the low value definitives, the stamps to be printed in (photo)gravure. This technique involved the transfer of a photograph to a copper printing cylinder by means of a chemical etch. First a glass negative is made. Using a step-and-repeat camera a glass positive is created bearing the number of images of the design (240 in this case) at actual stamp size. This is called a multi-positive. A paper-backed sheet of gelatine is exposed to light through a screen and the multi-positive plate recreating the image on the gelatine. More light - the harder the gelatine; no light and the gelatine remains soft. The gelatine is then applied to the cylinder and the paper backing stripped off. Bathing the cylinder in hot water washes away the unhardened gelatine and the image is then etched into the copper using iron perchloride, the iron penetrating the thinner parts of the gelatine more quickly than the thicker, creating a gradation of tones.

The resulting cells from the screen are squarish in shape, the deeper the cell the more ink it retains and therefore the darker the printed tone. During printing the cylinder is inked as it revolves, excess ink being removed by a "doctor blade" so that the ink remains only in the cells. When the paper meets the inked etch between the cylinder and an impression roller under very heavy pressure it withdraws the ink from the cells, each of which prints what looks like a minute dot.

As the essays for different values were approved, each design went

Arnold Machin watching his stamps being printed at Harrisons.

Machin's sketches for a first day cover.

through this process to create the printing cylinders. The end result produces an excellent tonal image, though lines are not sharp.

Issue

When it became obvious that a new design was finally in view thought turned to values and issue dates. An earlier exercise had attempted to reduce the number of denominations but this had not been carried through. A further detailed analysis of stamp usage provided the information required to plan the staged issue of the new definitive set. At a meeting on 10 December 1966 the number of values was reduced from 17 to 14 by eliminating several of the $^{1}/2$d denominations and the 1/3d which new postage rates had made unnecessary. The final values and colours were essayed between March and June.

At the beginning of March 1967 a provisional programme of issue dates was agreed for the definitive values in four stages over the next year, and then dates for Regional versions to follow [26]:

First day of sale	Denominations
5 June 1967	4d, 1/-, 1/9d
8 August 1967	3d, 9d, 1/6d
5 February 1968	$^{1}/2$d, 1d, 2d, 6d
1 April 1968	5d, 7d, 8d, 10d
10 June 1968	4d, 9d Regionals
5 August 1968	3d, 1/6d Regionals

The first three dates were kept. For the last batch the date was delayed until 1 July 1968 and the Regionals were postponed indefinitely, only to appear in decimal format.

Initial sketch, possibly by Stuart Rose, for the first day cover design.

First Day Cover

For the first time it was decided to treat the new definitive series in the same way as new commemorative or pictorial stamps. Issue dates would be announced in advance and a full first day cover service would be provided. A design was required for the cover. Naturally, the Post Office turned to Arnold Machin to provide one which would complement his stamp design, probably early in March 1967. At the same time, or as a result of sketches supplied, they enquired of the Home Office about the possibility of utilising the Royal Coat of Arms. Little exists in writing but the answer was clearly negative. Machin submitted various designs and two more sent on 28 March. These show rather elaborate heraldry-based designs with a lion or crowned shield. Tantalisingly, little more survives except a letter from Don Beaumont in reply.

"We have had a long look at all the designs you have done but have reluctantly decided, after advice from the Home Office, that we cannot use a design which features any kind of crown. There is bound to be some controversy from the general public should we use a crown based on 'imagination' and this is the kind of thing we wish to avoid.

We have settled on design No. 3 on the enclosed sheet of roughs.

Layout sketch for the first day cover.

5 June 1967. First
day cover for the
first three stamps,
signed by Arnold
Machin.

[no roughs now extant] What we would like you to do is eliminate the crown and substitute 'Definitive Issue'. We would have no objection to you reversing this with 'First day Cover' should you wish it. Also we wish to avoid any dates on the design since some of the stamps of the range will not be issued until next year." [27]

There is no record of a reply but it is unlikely that Machin would have agreed to these requests. Nevertheless, mention is still being made of work done by Machin in April, in relation to fees. However, the design used for the issued first day cover is a simple typographical arrangement. It seems more likely to have been sketched by Stuart Rose, Typographical Adviser to the Postmaster General. Artwork was sent to HMSO for production on 20 April. Different colours were used for the various issue dates.

No presentation packs were produced initially for the new definitives. However, as with previous stamp issues, Short wanted to present examples of the new stamps to a very limited number of VIPs (such as The Queen, Princess Margaret, the Prime Minister, former postmasters general and members of the

Stamp Advisory Committee). Special cards were designed (probably by Stuart Rose) and produced with the stamps affixed within. These were created for each of the issue dates.

The Second Definitive Issue of Postage Stamps of the Reign of Her Majesty Queen Elizabeth II 5th June 1967

Payment

Work had continued throughout 1966 with no mention of fee. At this time Machin was teaching at the Royal Academy, which provided a small, basic salary. The question of copyright prompted the Post Office to address the question urgently. Discussions with the Solicitor's Department of the Post Office made it clear that the original commission was no longer valid but that nothing had replaced it. A memo dated 6 April stated that the situation was unprecedented.

"We have repeatedly asked Mr Machin to let us have some idea of what he might consider a reasonable fee for the project. After many reminders he has suggested a figure of between £4,000 and £5,000.

At first glance this seems to be excessive. We have, however, had a word with Mr Grant of the Council of Industrial Design about this, asking for his views. He took the following facts into consideration:-

a Machin has been working on the project since November, 1965, and is continuing to work on it, e.g. he is liaising with Bradbury Wilkinsons for the recess version and will probably be asked to do a stylised head for the special stamp series;

b That the fee of a top class sculptor is in the region of 7 guineas per hour;

c That Machin has undoubtedly had to refuse other lucrative commissions over the period he has been working on this project;

d That Mr Machin's expenses, throughout his commission, have been far greater than would be the case for a normal stamp design project." [28]

DEFINITIVE POSTAGE STAMPS SERIES

4d Denomination - 1967

It was thus decided to offer Machin a fee of £4,500 to cover the whole of the work, including any subsequent work such as first day cover design, a recess head and a possible head for special stamps. He agreed and received the amount in May with copyright in the original bas relief model and the designs based on it vested in the Crown. However, he noted that any further work on the model would have to be treated separately. [29]

A note at this time from D M Walbank, Senior Legal Assistant, gave legal advice about copyright. Within a short summary of the history of the design he stated that "it is understood from Beaumont that none of the photographs prepared by John Vickers Studio or John Hedgecoe Limited were used in connection with Mr Machin's portrayal in bas-relief." [30] And thus no further payments to them were required.

Press Conference & Acclaim

The Postmaster General, Edward (Ted) Short, decided to hold a press conference to announce details of the new definitive series on Monday 6 March in Post Office Headquarters. The example to be shown was the completed 4d value. A long speech was drafted by officials but decisively cut by the appropriately named PMG, omitting a lot of background and any reference to his predecessor.

"As part of the development on postage stamps we felt that a new definitive series of stamps were called for. The existing set is attractive in many ways but in a style which is now-a-days outmoded. We had, of course, to have as the main feature of the new series a portrait of the reigning monarch. The current definitive series carries a 3/4 photograph of the Monarch. This particular portrait has, however, when used for the larger sized special issues, inhibited the rest of the design. The Advisory Committee on Stamp Design set up by the Council of Industrial Design advised that our stamps could be improved if the Sovereign's head were in profile instead of 3/4 face. They pointed out that in the majority of stamps the objects represented are in a single plane; and to show the head in 3/4 face introduces an element of depth which it is difficult to combine with the flat design of other parts of the stamps. To meet this point we have used in a number of our recent special issues a profile cameo portrait adapted from the design on our coinage. But we did not feel that this was the answer for the definitive series.

After months of extremely hard work by Mr Arnold Machin and the printers, Messrs Harrison and Sons Ltd., a design was evolved which in my opinion will be one of the classics of stamp history. This design was produced by photographing a sculpture in bas-relief modelled by Mr Machin and adding only the value indicator. Unlike the existing designs it has no national emblems and with the agreement of the Inland Revenue Department both the words 'Postage' and 'Revenue' are omitted. The result is a classical simplicity of design." [31]

The accompanying press release noted that The Queen had expressly requested the olive brown sepia colour, and that the stamps would be printed on unwatermarked paper, all overprinted with phosphor lines (for machine readability) for the first time. It ended by saying that Machin had been chosen on the advice of the COID Stamp Advisory Committee, without mentioning that this had just been disbanded. A short biography of Machin was provided ending with the fact that he "is married to an artist and they have a 17 year old son still at school." [32]

1   P52/71 op cit

2   POST 122/10720 op cit. memo 31 October 1966

3   POST 122/10712 op cit

4   POST 122/10720 op cit

5   ibid

6   **Machin, Arnold** op cit pp137/8

7   30 March 1987. letter from Ken Scrimgeour (Harrisons) to Don Staddon

8   POST 122/10720 op cit

9   POST 122/10708 Postage Stamps: Stamp Design Policy. New look. Essays by Harrisons

10 ibid

11 **Machin, Arnold** op cit p138

12 POST 122/12377 Postage Stamps: Permanent Series: Queen Elizabeth II – Second Issue – New Designs – Low Value Range

13 Press & Broadcast Notice PB 54 6 March 1967

14 POST 122/12377 op cit

15 ibid

16 POST 122/10712 op cit

17 ibid

18 ibid

19 ibid

20 ibid

21 ibid

22 14 March 1967. letter from Harrisons to Machin referring to colours of essays

23 POST 122/10712 op cit

24 POST 52/370 New (Low Value) definitive stamps 1967.

25 ibid

26 POST 122/10721 Postage Stamps. Stamp Design Policy: New look. New definitive and regional stamps issue dates. Also POST 52/370 op cit.

27 POST122/12377 op cit

28 POST 122/10722 Postage Stamps. Stamp Design Policy: New look. Arnold Machin's profile portrait of the Queen. Copyright of the design.

29 POST 122/12377 op cit

30 POST 122/10722 op cit

31 POST 122/12377 op cit

32 ibid

1 0

With the programme for the low value definitives well advanced, concern turned to the high values. Current designs dated from 1955 and featured castles from the four countries, together with the Wilding portrait. The contract to print these was held by Bradbury Wilkinson Ltd, with printing being in intaglio (recess). Unfortunately, with regard to the new designs required, official sources are sparse and a number of gaps exist in the story.

On 8 March 1967, what was described as "the working model of the Queen's head for the new definitive issue" [1] was sent by Harrisons to Bradbury Wilkinsons in New Malden, Surrey for them to begin experiments – presumably the photograph of the version used against a full background (with the missing pearl). Subsequently, this proved inadequate. On 31 March the printers informed postal officials that "they had had a long look at this and decided that it would not suit the line-engraved process and would be inferior to what they could produce from their own photographs of the Machin plaque." It was agreed that they should "concentrate on their own particular line." [2]

However, initial ideas were not of an engraved version of the head alone. Bradbury Wilkinson were eager to provide multicolour essays. At the time the line-engraved (intaglio) process could only cope with two colours. On the other hand, Bradbury Wilkinson had a process which combined offset litho printing over line-engraving.

This seemed promising and it was agreed to try it out. The Post Office asked the printers on 10 March to provide essays incorporating the new head:

a   using the existing castle motif designs (in the current colours) and

b   in variations of the current four values in multi-colour designs (recess/litho) using your own suggested designs (same size as 'Castle' stamps) [3]

The word "Postage" was to be omitted. No mention was made of a single, large engraved head, at least at this date. A memo to the Postmaster General, undated but from about this period in mid March, reiterates the printers' proposals but amplifies the requirements. The current Castles designs have now been dropped to be replaced with "single heads similar to the low values" as well as the suggested new designs by the printers.

Sketches by Machin for pictorial high values featuring a print of Glencoe and the royal coat of arms.

"We would suggest that for the new high value series we should have fresh designs while still retaining the regional motif, i.e. separate stamps illustrating some specific aspect relating to England, Scotland, Northern Ireland and Wales. Artists could be asked to submit designs of their own choice — as in 1955 — but within a specific sphere, e.g. architecture, customs, beauty spots, ancient monuments etc." [4]

At the outset it was emphasised that Machin was to be involved and consulted in the use of his head, that the printers should work in "very close co-operation" with him and that "his personal views about the engraved head should very much be borne in mind". [5] No correspondence seems to have survived but three sketches produced by Machin have. Two are versions of an engraved print of the same view of Glencoe in the Scottish highlands, with an engraved Machin head beside it. The third is a stamp-size mock-up using a gravure Machin head beside an illustration of the royal coat of arms.

Both Machin and Bradbury Wilkinson were satisfied with the first engraving of the head. Approval was to be sought from the PMG when it was stated that arrangements were in hand to produce a larger head like that in the series of previous reigns. Only mock-ups were then available but when the meeting with the PMG was to take place both Machin and Mr Burge of Bradbury Wilkinson wanted to be present.

Designs produced for the printers were by Michael Goaman. One design featured light coming through trees in a forest; the other HMS *Victory*. These were essayed in various colours in the combined recess/litho processes, with engraved Machin heads of differing sizes, and a total of 21 were ready by July.

PMG Unimpressed

There was a meeting at the House of Commons on 24 July between Edward Short, the PMG, Arnold Machin and Mr Burge to discuss the line-engraved essays. A short memo recorded the PMG's dissatisfaction. Given his enthusiasm for the unadorned Machin head on the low values, this is perhaps not surprising.

"Postmaster General was not enthusiastic about the results so far and asked for further essays of the head to be produced, based on the photogravure version.

[He] indicated that the new essays should be the same size as the first high value series of the reign of George VI. The designs should show only the profile portrait, the various national symbols i.e., rose, thistle, shamrock and daffodil in the four corners, and the value, centre, under the profile." [6]

The standard values of 2s 6d, 5s, 10s and £1 were to be retained and each denomination was to be in one colour, although a selection of colours were to be proofed from which a final choice could be made. Short wanted to show the essays to The Queen at a Privy Council at Balmoral in September, with the aim of issuing the high value series in August 1968.

Within days, two essays were created from photographic enlargements of the 4d definitive, one with national emblems in each corner, and one without the emblems. The latter was selected. [7]

Re-photographing the cast

During March Bradbury Wilkinson examined the "working model" from Harrisons in order to engrave the head and concluded that this was inadequate for their purposes. This meant that new photographs would have to be taken to provide greater highlights in the modelling to enable the engraver to produce a satisfactory rendering. Several photographs exist of the

A selection of photographs by Bradbury Wilkinson of the blackened plaster cast.

Some of the Bradbury Wilkinson photographs of the plaster cast used for pastel coloured low values

cast used for full background stamps (with two lines in the hair and missing pearl). The background of the cast has by now been blackened and the lighting is often harsh from various angles. Quite how many were taken is unclear but 18 were later archived.

Strangely, a few photographs also exist, from the same series, of the other cast (full pearls and one line in the hair) as used for low value definitives with pastel, gradated backgrounds. This cast had not been blackened. Thus it would seem that during April two different plaster casts were taken to Bradbury Wilkinson for photography under the supervision of Arnold Machin. In retrospect, this reinforces the argument about photography at Harrisons for the low value stamps. It is abundantly clear that two different casts were photographed and no single print was used for the resulting stamps. For the high values the printers later made clear that no one photograph was used as their source and that the engraved design came from an amalgam of several studies. [8]

Proofs and Printing

Two engravings of the head were prepared by one of Bradbury Wilkinson's two master craftsmen, R. G. Godbehear, assisted by A. Dow. A second master craftsman J. G. Heymes, was responsible for engraving the background and lettering. [9] The two head engravings were labelled "A" and "B" differing in

September 1967.
First proofs of high
values Head A

BRADBURY, WILKINSON & COMPANY, LTD.
NEW MALDEN, SURREY.
ENGLAND·

the appearance of the corsage and face, particularly the cheekbones and chin.

In September, essays were prepared from both head engravings with altered denominations on head "B" reflecting criticism of the value tablet. All showed the £1 value in four very dark colours including dark green. These were shown to The Queen in October and the printers were informed of the results in a letter of 30 October.

"The Queen carefully examined both sets of designs you submitted and has signified a definite preference for the accompanying specimens." [10] *[head "A"]*

Colours now had to be decided for the four values and Bradbury Wilkinson were asked to produce a series of essays.

"a. in different shades of the current 2s 6d brown, 5s red, 10s blue and £1 black; and

b. in alternative shades of colours agreed between yourselves and Mr Machin." [11]

500 sheets of paper (11" x 9") were supplied for "proving". The only die of set "A" available was the £1. This was altered to modify the value tablet, now lined, and then proofed in 23 colours supplied on 19 December. No indication is given as to any influence from Machin but all the colours bar one (dark green) were in shades of the current colours, but much richer and more colourful than before. These were shown to The Queen the following month (though whether a selection or

September 1967. Proofs of Head B (not preferred)

all is not clear) and four were approved for colour alone on 25 January 1968 (Nos. 5, 8, 20 and 21). The colours chosen were:

2s 6d	Peat Brown
5s	Raspberry Red
10s	Sapphire Blue
£1	Blue/black

January 1968.
Colours approved
for the four high
values

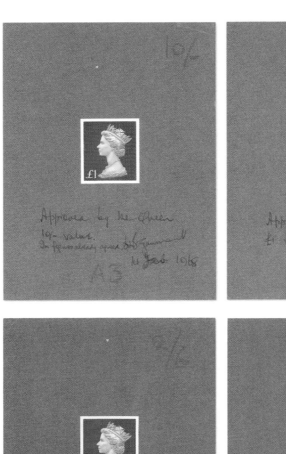
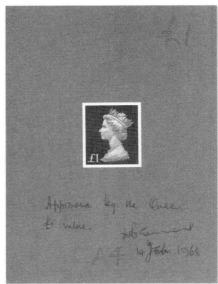
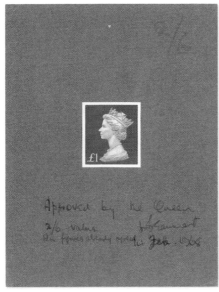
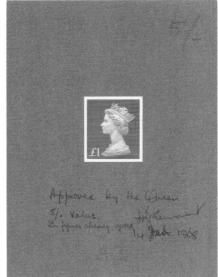

New dies now had to be engraved for the other values and these were ready and proofed in the correct colours on 20 March. These designs were shown to the newly reconstituted Stamp Advisory Committee [12] on 10 April for information only. In general they were "pleased" with the stamps but thought the numerals could be improved. They also felt that the background colours could be richer. [13] Approval for colour and design came on 30 April. [14]

30 April 1968. Proofs approved for colour and design.

Traditionally in creating a plate for recess (or line-engraving) printing, the master die for each value was engraved in reverse on a small steel plate which was then hardened. This image was then transferred on to a steel roller or molette under great pressure where it was right-facing but standing proud in relief. After again being hardened the image was then "rocked" on to the printing plate in the format required for printing (in this case in four panes of 40). Once again after being hardened, and now with the image once again in reverse, the plates were curved to be attached to a cylinder. Ink was retained in the grooves and subsequently stood proud on the printed sheet. Great pressure was required at each stage of the operation.

Original head die roller

Master or "Key" die
for the £1 value (in
reverse)

Despite having great experience of engraving dies and creating printing plates Bradbury Wilkinson failed to produce ones of acceptable quality, which meant that the issue date had to be postponed from September 1968, as proposed, until March 1969. An internal memo to the Postmaster General explained:

"Line-engraving is a rather more lengthy and expensive process than photogravure and is therefore more suitable for the smaller printing runs of the high values. The reason given for using it was formerly security, but the real reason now is that it gives stamps of a special character which are liked by many philatelists.

The design has recently been publicly shown, the first day of sale being given as 9th September. This should have given ample time, indeed much longer than is usually necessary, for printing and distribution ...

However, a number of unforeseen technical problems then cropped up concerning the etching of the master die, the design and the paper to be used. The first plate attempts were unsuccessful. We have now just seen proofs of the second and they are quite unsatisfactory because of poor colour and blotchiness.

The printer favours use of a different etching technique which he is fairly sure will overcome the present difficulties and will produce stamps up to approved essay standards. We certainly cannot issue stamps of the standard he has so far produced in trials and only agree to what the printer suggests." [15]

New transfer rollers were created in July 1968 in order to produce new plates. Eventually, proof sheets from all four plates (160 set) were approved at the beginning of January 1969 (2 January – 2s 6d, 10s; 9 January - 5s, £1). [16] Issue date was now 5 March.

Printing plate (4) for the original £1 value

Paper

On the assumption that there would be no problems with printing, arrangements for the supply of paper were made in February 1968. As with the low values it was to be unwatermarked

Small photographic
sketch by Machin
with a laurel
wreath replacing
the diadem

for the first time. A detailed specification was provided by the Post Office Supplies Department.

"It is necessary for unwatermarked paper to be supplied in coated and gummed sheets. As Messrs Harrison and Sons Ltd now provide the coated and gummed paper on which they print Unified [Machin] stamps it is desirable that, to ensure uniformity of paper, coating and gum, they should be asked to supply the sheets required for High Value stamps." [17]

The contract was to supply 1,125 reams of coated rectangular sheets ($21^7/_{16}$ inches by $16^1/_2$ inches) "the paper to be similar in all respects to that provided for Unified stamps" with PVA gum. When the delay set in with the preparation of the new printing plates for the Machin high values further supplies of the old Castles high values became necessary. These were produced on the new Harrisons unwatermarked paper (sometimes termed Post Office paper by philatelists).

Commemorative Head

Photograph of
the original plaster
cast for the
commemorative
head

After work had started on the high values it was realised that the standard accepted version of the head could not be used at smaller size on commemorative or pictorial stamps. When Short wrote to The Queen he explained:

"We found in fact that when the exact profile used on the definitives was reduced in size it lost much of its attractiveness. In particular the tiara [sic] took on a very spikey appearance and the profile itself became too sharp." [18]

5 December 1967. Essays of the commemorative head, large, medium and small size

So Machin had been asked to produce another simplified head. George York wrote to him from Harrisons on 25 July 1967.

"I have been instructed by the Post Office to ask whether you are prepared to produce new heads of the Queen suitable for use on commemorative and pictorial issues.

It seems to me that two types of head will be required. One that will be suitable for special issues such as British Birds, and British Flora, and a smaller type of head probably to be used as a silhouette, which will be suitable for pictorial issues such as British Paintings, and the new style Christmas stamp, which you have already seen." [19]

Machin proceeded to simplify his design by replacing the diadem with a laurel wreath and adding ribbons at the back. As usual this began life as a worked photographic drawing and was then translated into a plaster cast. Again the background of the cast was blackened and photographs taken as

POST CARD

POSTAGE POSTAGE

4ᴰ

This Single Postcard was taken in the presence of the Post Office Control Officer at the factory of Messrs. McCorquodale & Co. Ltd. at Wolverton for registration of the first print with a 4d. stamp.

. . . .
P & SD, Supplies Division,
Stamp Depot.

. . . .
Chief Executive Officer

...8......10......1968

before, with bromides at different sizes both showing the relief detail and in silhouette. From these, essays were created by Harrisons in a number of different formats.

The essays showed the commemorative head alone, often in a metallic colour (gold, silver, copper and bronze) against a solid colour background. There were three sizes, large, medium and small, often combined with embossing. They were supplied by Harrisons on 5 December 1967 in preparation for a meeting the following day of postal officials, York and Machin with the PMG.

Apart from minor detail it was agreed that the revised head was suitable and Short wrote to the Palace asking for The Queen's approval – "the two smaller sizes in particular are typical of what would be used on special issue stamps." [20]

A letter came back the following day giving The Queen's agreement:

"*Her Majesty was most interested to see these and thinks them an improvement on those in present use.*" [21] *[the Gillick head]*

Essays were trialled with designs of two current special stamps of 1967 at different sizes, both in gold and white out and also with embossing. The first time it appeared on issued stamps was on the 1968 British Bridges set (where interestingly it was used both left- and right-facing for the first time).

A white silhouette version was also created based on a photograph, for use on the 1968 Christmas airletter.

Postal Stationery Embossed Die

Postal stationery also had to be brought into line with the new head. For several items such as postcards and letter cards a half-tone letterpress version of the stamp design was used with added lettering. The original sketch consists of a cut-down (gravure) stamp with the legend POSTAGE/REVENUE and 4d around it. Later the REVENUE was dropped.

Electrotype created by the Royal Mint from the stationery plaster cast

However, for envelopes and registered envelopes an embossed die was required. The Royal Mint created relief stationery dies for the Post Office and their requirements were different from those of flat printing. Machin would have been well

Left First head
punch (without
value) from
Machin's stationery
plaster cast

Right 19 December
1968. Die for 5d
embossed
envelope.

1969. Registration
copy of the first
embossed envelope
(issued 7 October).

This Postage Envelope, type 'A' 5d was taken
in the presence of the Post Office Control
Officer at the factory of Messrs McCorquodale
& Co Ltd at Wolverton for registration of the
first print of this item with the Machin Head
design stamp.

....
Chief Executive Officer

..............7o...1.º1969

Initials of Control Officer
Supplies Dept
Stamp Depot

aware of these from the period when he was working on his head for the coinage which first came out in Britain about this time. The Mint required a cast to an 8 inch diameter and Brian Sproat from the Post Office contacted Machin in May 1968 to ask him if he could create this. It was required urgently and so a fee of 500 guineas was agreed. [22]

Delivery was required by July and although Machin asked for detailed background information about the Mint's requirements it was suggested that he contact their Chief Engraver (W. J. Newman) direct. The cast was produced and supplied as requested and Machin was paid on 29 August. Detail of the diadem was much more simple, even rough, but this did not matter as it was more the outline which was important for colourless embossing out of a solid background.

An octagonal design was created by Stuart Rose based on this in 4d and 5d versions for envelopes and 3/5d for registered envelopes. Initially, the design bore the same legend as the postcards. However, a letter from Sproat to Rose on 10 June explained that "we have now discovered that 'cut out' embossed and impressed stamps … cannot be used for revenue purposes." He was asked to amend his die accordingly. The first die was ready on 19 December 1968. It was not until October 1969, however, that the first item was issued to the public.

Extensions delayed

By this time the new head had been extended to most of the range of postal items produced by the Post Office. With the impending change to decimal currency, work now concentrated on that, with many definitive colour trials resulting from some difficulties with the chosen colours (the 4d olive sepia brown chosen by The Queen had to be changed to red to avoid problems with sorting machinery). The only major item not yet tackled, the Regional or Country stamps, had to wait for decimalisation before they were issued, with symbols designed by Jeffery Matthews.

1   POST 52/371 Correspondence – New High value postage stamps

2   MD/CO/109 Permanent series: Queen Elizabeth II - Second Issue New Definitives, High Value Range

3   ibid

4   ibid

5   POST 52/371 op cit

6   ibid

7   **Staddon, D.** "The Genesis of the Machin Design" Part 8 *British Philatelic Bulletin* pp 204-5 May 1987

8   2 March 1978. Letter from Bradbury Wilkinson to National Postal Museum

9   ibid

10   MD/CO/109 op cit

11   ibid

12   Now under P.O. chairmanship (George Downes). Professor Guyatt and Sir Paul Reilly survived from the previous SAC. Other external members were: B. Batsford and G. Rogers (both MPs); Kenneth F Chapman and Ronald A G Lee (from the philatelic world); Anthony Lousada and Herbert Spencer (designers); Stuart Rose; and Mrs L. Pearce (representing the public).

13   POST 54/17 *Postmaster General's new Stamp Advisory Committee minutes*

14   POST 52/1054 High value postage

15   MD/CO/109 op cit, George Downes 23 July 1968

16   POST 52/1054 op cit

17   POST 52/371 op cit

18   MD/CO/757/A Design – New Machin commemorative head

19   25 July 1967. R.F. York to Arnold Machin

20   MD/CO/757/A op cit 14 December 1967

21   ibid

22   13 May 1968. B T Sproat to Arnold Machin

11

"Her Majesty is very content with the Machin effigy and thinks that a work of real quality is required if this is to be replaced."

Once achieved, the Machin design continued in use successfully for many years with several changes of value, decimalisation and various revisions of colour standards. It was also used in different formats and printed by a variety of techniques. Yet, the basic head had remained the same. However, in March 1981 a proposal was put to the "Posts and Girobank Board", as it was by then called, to introduce a new design for definitive stamps to mark the 30th anniversary of the coronation which would fall in June 1983. What proved to be a very optimistic timetable was attached detailing how this could be achieved. The Queen's approval in principle was to be sought at the outset, a photographer agreed and the Stamp Advisory Committee (reconstituted in 1968) consulted. Essay and printing stages were scheduled so that the stamps could go on sale some two years later. Over a much longer period the exercise was to prove impossible.

Right at the outset Barry Robinson, Design Adviser to the Post Office, entered a caveat.

April 1982.
Photograph by
Lord Snowdon.

"We must accept that our present range is probably the best definitive range in the world and with so many unknown factors, we cannot rely on being able to improve upon the design. The present Machin head is not an illustration of the Queen, but a symbol. That symbol is as relevant and identifiable today as it was when first issued." [2]

Nevertheless, Post Office Chairman, Ron Dearing, wrote to the Palace on 30 July 1981 asking for agreement in principle to go ahead. The reply from William Heseltine (Deputy Private Secretary to The Queen) was couched in diplomatic terms but nevertheless made quite clear The Queen's views.

"Her Majesty is prepared to give consideration to the issue of a further definitive issue of postage stamps for use in the 30th year of her reign. Before giving a definite reply to your proposal, however, The Queen would very much like to know who you had in mind to produce the new effigy. It is a difficult thing to do and Her Majesty is very content with the Machin effigy and thinks that a work of real quality is required if this is to be replaced." [3]

After some delay, Barry Robinson wrote an internal memo on how to respond to this.

"In drafting the Chairman's reply to the palace we must emphasise how aware we are that a work of real quality is required to replace the Machin effigy, and that we do not profess to having arrived at the final solution at this point in time.

We can say however that the final result would be a 'portrait'. As yet we are uncertain whether it will be a photographic, illustrative or a sculpted portrait.

We propose that our first course of action would be to ask Her Majesty to agree to an initial photographic session with, perhaps, Lord Snowdon." [4]

Dearing wrote following the lines indicated and received The Queen's agreement in principle for work to go ahead, her Private Secretary to contact Lord Snowdon with regard to the photography required. "She is equally content that the effigy on the new stamps will have no relationship to that which appears on the coinage." [5]

June 1982. First drawing by Rory Matthews

Jeffery Matthews, the well-known stamp designer (especially of royal themes), was then briefed to undertake the project. Jeffery studied earlier portraits of monarchs on stamps and noted that in the main these were drawn portraits after photographic studies. He thought this approach would be the best way of achieving the varied requirements of the new portrait.

"The skilfully drawn portrait captures the many facets of character in a composite of expressions, and with a subtle degree of stylization can symbolize the subject in a likeness which is acceptable over a considerable period of time." [6]

A drawn portrait also allowed the designer greater control over the space with values being more easily accommodated. Possibilities previously used were 3/4 and full profile. The alternative was full-face, which Matthews strongly favoured.

First Attempts

In March 1982 Lord Snowdon was asked to take a series of photographs of The Queen, views ranging from full profile to full-face. Over 200 shots were supplied the following month. One full-face version was retouched by Terry

Boxall (a retoucher favoured by Snowdon) to clarify the features and it was agreed that Rory Matthews (Jeffery Matthews' son) should prepare a drawn portrait based upon these Snowdon photographic studies. His first drawing was submitted on 10 June.

From this drawing Jeffery Matthews then prepared two pieces of artwork with different tone backgrounds and specifications for a number of variations. Essays based on these were to be prepared by Harrisons in gravure in salmon pink and grey green, the colours of the current $2^{1}/2$p and 13p definitives. At the same time essays were also to be produced from the original Snowdon photograph and the retouched version for comparison.

1982. First essays in salmon pink

First essays (a total of 14 types in each colour) were received on 24 August and apparently confirmed the supposition that a drawn portrait was likely to give a more satisfactory result. Amendments were agreed and carried out by the printers to produce a second set of essays. These were proofed (10 in all) in

7   8   13   14   11   12

1982. First essays in grey green

the same colours as before, but also in steel blue and maroon, and a new large format was produced for high values. When Lord Snowdon was shown the first essays he unsurprisingly expressed a preference for the photographic approach.

9A   9B   10A   10B

7 October 1982.
Second essays in
steel blue

In November 1982, the Post Office Chairman, Ron Dearing, was shown the work to date. He felt that more than one photograph should be used so that The Queen could be offered a choice. As a result further photographs were considered and Rory Matthews amended his first portrait. A third set of essays was then produced in grey green and maroon, including more photographs from the Snowdon session.

"Regarding the two additional photographic portraits, both Barry Robinson and Jeffery Matthews felt that these but served to show slight variations in the pose and confirmed the inappropriateness of a smiling portrait for an image which must stand the test of time." [7]

November 1982.
Amended drawing
by Rory Matthews

About this time The Queen enquired what progress was being made and a set of the third essays was submitted to her. Her reaction was described as "most interested and encouraging" but she had made some comments on detail. For these Barry Robinson was invited to the Palace to see William Heseltine. He confirmed the view that the retouched photograph was unacceptable, that the timeless quality of a drawn portrait as opposed to a photograph was desirable, but some reservation was expressed with regard to the likeness in the experimental drawing; also that "a hint of a smile might be appropriate". [8] Time was now pressing if the original schedule was to be kept but it transpired that the Palace attached no particular significance to the coronation anniversary of 2 June 1983. Timetables were therefore lengthened and a possible issue date was delayed to 1984. The priority was to produce an acceptable stamp.

At this point essays were shown to the Stamp Advisory Committee for the first time. The essays shown on 27 January 1983 were based on photographs by Lord Snowdon and consisted of:

    a. unretouched photographs

    b. retouched photographs

    c. drawing based on photographs

These were rejected. One of the designer members of the Committee, Professor Herbert Spencer, "thought that approaches should be made to artists with experience of painting the Queen, and that it was a mistake to commission an artist on the basis of photographs". [9]

Nevertheless, it was agreed that the Design Adviser, Barry Robinson would consult various artists and obtain a consensus of opinion on the best method. The Palace would then be approached again on the agreed concept.

December 1982. Third essays in grey green shown to the Stamp Advisory Committee

Drawing

Retouched photograph

Unretouched photograph

Second Attempt with new portraits

New artists chosen were John Sargeant, Brian Sanders, Timothy Whidborne, all asked to produce full-face portraits based on Snowdon's photographs. Rory Matthews was also asked to provide a new portrait.

"This choice of names was nicely balanced in that it gave patronage to: a young artist (Rory Matthews); a portraitist who had already received Royal patronage (Timothy Whidborne); an illustrator in the commercial field (John Sargeant); and a tried stamp designer (Brian Sanders)." [10]

They responded in late February and early March 1983 with a tight pencil drawing (Matthews), a loose pencil drawing (Sargeant), a watercolour (Sanders) and an oil painting (Whidborne). All were essayed in the same colour (dark green) for a clear comparison, from April to October that year.

From left to right
1983. Second pencil drawing by Rory Matthews and essays

1983. Pencil drawing by John Sargeant and essay

1983. Oil painting by Timothy Whidborne and essay

1983. Watercolour by Brian Sanders and essays

JOHN SARGEANT

Thereafter little happened until January the following year when a meeting took place at Harrisons, the printers, to recapitulate, work on essays having been deferred. It was decided to continue working on the portraits by Rory Matthews and Timothy Whidborne but not the others "it being felt that Harrisons had already taken the reproduction of the other two portraits by John Sargeant and Brian Sanders as far as was necessary to demonstrate the results obtainable from the variety of artistic approach which these portraits represented." [11]

About this time Czeslaw Slania, the famous stamp engraver, was working on engraving the designs for the mailcoach anniversary stamps which appeared in

TIMOTHY WHIDBORNE

BRIAN SANDERS

1984. As Robinson was visiting Slania in Sweden in connection with that it was agreed that he ask him to retouch Snowdon's photograph and try that. Essays

were produced from the result in March and April but showed no great improvement. An engraved version was also created and tried out in larger format.

In July 1984, the Stamp Advisory Committee rejected all the essays of the four portraits based on the Snowdon photographs. It was agreed that these designs did not provide a basis for further development.

1983. Engraving by Czeslaw Slania.

June 1985.
Bicoloured essays of
the Machin head.

	light head	dark head	light head	dark head	
light background	B1.3	B1.4	B3.3	B3.4	light background
dark background	B2.3	B2.4	B4.3	B4.4	dark background

Third Attempt with Machin variants

A small Working Party was then set up to consider new designs and after two meetings decided to work with bi-coloured versions of the Machin head. The first versions were in dark green or dark blue with the head in either "warm" or "cool" grey. These were considered in June when other colours were required. Keeping the head in black, six background colours were provided: dark blue, dark green, dark brown, crimson, sand and ash pink.

Essays were printed on 16 July 1985 in two versions, with or without an outline or "halo" to the head in preparation for submission to the SAC.

The full SAC met on 18 July 1985 but views differed, largely between those who were also members of the

Working Party and those who were not and were thus seeing the results for the first time. Most thought the changes marginal and the colours too harsh, but agreed that the symbolic Machin head should be retained.

"Dr [Jean] Alexander was disappointed with the proposals, which she saw as only a slight modification that could not be regarded as a new series. She accepted that the Machin head was symbolic, and this got over the problem of ageing the head, but she would like to see a more dramatic change than this. She thought the new design should show the head and neck only, and not the shoulders: this would be seen as a major change." [12]

Fourth Attempt with Machin cut-offs

Action on removing the lower neck and shoulders of The Queen's head was initially deferred pending a definite decision to proceed, but this came in September and Jeffery Matthews was asked to develop matters further. As a result he produced an exploratory range of 18 photographic essays with Machin heads with differing positions of cut at the neck, to be seen by a meeting of the Working Party on 26 September. Any adaptation of the Machin head would obviously mean negotiation with Arnold Machin and so

September 1985. Exploratory designs by Jeffery Matthews with varying cuts to the neck of the Machin head.

September 1985.
Exploratory designs
by Jeffery Matthews
with varying cuts to
the neck of the
Machin head.

Barry Robinson and Jeffery Matthews travelled to Staffordshire to meet him
on 23 October.

What transpired, after a subsequent telephone conversation, was recorded in
an angry exchange of letters, worth quoting in full as it has informed matters
to this day. Machin wrote to Robinson on 1 November.

"Dear Barry

After our meeting on 23rd October and the following telephone conversation you can no longer be in any doubt that I am very disturbed by the fact that you have produced designs for the alteration of the Definitive Stamp without consulting me, and have presented them to the Stamp Committee.

During our meeting both you and Jeffery Matthews attempted to coerce me into accepting a proposal which involved the removal of the lower half of the portrait of H.M. the Queen in order to make space for the numeral, and this horrifies me.

You will forgive me, then, if this together with the fact that you have already produced essays of another variation at the printing works leads me to believe that it was your intention to present me with a fait accompli.

During our telephone conversation your argument was that the altering of the portrait was the easiest part of the exercise and that the adding of the numeral presented the real problem; this makes me realise that you have no conception of how the quality of the first stamp was achieved.

Apart from the ethics, it was a nonsense to invite someone else in the alteration of my work when you see what I was able to achieve and what a phenomenal success the Definitive Stamp has been.

The only way to produce a revised version is (1) to adjust the model if necessary (2) new photography (3) colour trials at the printing works, and no-one else but myself can do this.

This is how the first stamp was evolved and it is the only way it can be done now if the same high quality is to be maintained.

All that is required is the will to produce the finest possible stamp, and if we agree on that and work together amicably you have ample evidence, by looking at the early editions of the Definitive Stamp, that this can be achieved." [13]

After a few days Robinson replied, clearly equally angry:

"Dear Mr Machin

I am sorry that my visit to you on 23 October and a subsequent telephone conversation has left a situation of serious misunderstanding.

Since I clearly have failed to make the point in speaking to you, let me attempt to confirm it in writing.

I was charged with the task of considering all possibilities for producing a totally new definitive stamp. Not altering the existing design but a complete replacement from suitable artists who might work in photographic, watercolour, oils, pencil or even computer graphic origination. Jeffery Matthews, because of his high standards of design and a day to day experience of the operational requirements of the business, was commissioned to help me make a broad study of the whole problem.

Arnold Machin and Barry Robinson in 1987.

Periodically, we reported progress and decisions made to a small working party of SAC members. In recognition of the quality of the original stamp it was at a recent one of these meetings where we finally got the agreement to consider how the significant operational problems could possibly be accommodated retaining the existing head.

That is where we are today. No designs have been 'produced'. The work shown to you by Jeffery

29 June 1987. Late essays comparing Machin cut-offs with Rory Matthews designs.

25 November 1987. Landscape essays of the Machin head.

Matthews has been seen by no more than seven people. They were very preliminary thoughts on paper with the sole purpose of consulting you and seeking your views. You were not coerced or presented with a fait accompli and the very reason we were looking in that direction was because we appreciated the quality of the original stamp.

I very much regret that we seem to have reached a situation where you seem to believe we are on the verge of production and you have not been consulted. Viewed against the background of my broad terms of reference you were consulted at the earliest possible time.

I cannot commit The Post Office to accepting the continued use of the present head. It could, for a variety of reasons, decide to take some entirely different course. What I will commit The Post Office to is the fact that there will be no amendments made to the present bas-relief without your involvement and agreement. If and when we reach this stage I would like to think we could proceed in a positive and understanding manner." [14]

Although some designs continued to be essayed for about two years (mainly Regional designs) this was really the end of the search to replace the Machin. They had failed in the attempt to surpass, or remotely equal, the timeless classic. No work of "real quality" had emerged despite several years' work and considerable expense.

However, some time later, two different formats did appear which came directly from this experimental work – the double head Penny Black definitives of 1990 and the landscape versions of 1993, both designed by Jeffery Matthews.

1 5 August 1981. William Heseltine to Ron Dearing (P.O. Chairman). MKD/CJ/1048

2 ibid

3 ibid

4 ibid 22 September 1981. Barry Robinson to John Mackay

5 ibid 4 November 1981. William Heseltine to Ron Dearing.

6 ibid September/October 1982

7 ibid 12 December 1982

8 ibid 22 December 1982.

9 MKD/AN/1678 New Design for Definitive Stamps

10 MKD/CJ/1048 op cit

11 ibid

12 POST 54/23 Stamp Advisory Committee minutes, 1985

13 1 November 1985. Arnold Machin to Barry Robinson

14 12 November 1985. Barry Robinson to Arnold Machin

POSTSCRIPT

Machin at the 1987
NPM exhibition with
Sir Ron Dearing
(centre) and author
(second right)

For me, the Penny Black, the world's first postage stamp, is also the world's greatest and most beautiful. Although highly complex, it has a classic simplicity and has become a symbol of the entire Victorian era. It had no precedent, but it does have a worthy successor.

Arnold Machin's sculpture is the modern equivalent of the Penny Black. It too has become an icon, a symbol of monarchy and of the United Kingdom, something which was instantly recognised when the design was first published. As with the Penny Black the simplicity of Machin's design is more

The Machin
The Making of a Masterpiece
A Royal Mail book of stamps

apparent than real, and was the result of a vast amount of effort. Interestingly, both stamps originated in work for coins and medals and both resulted from the highest craftsmanship of the day. Looking at Machin's portrait of The Queen today you do not think of the 1960s. It has not dated, as so many aspects of fashion do. It is timeless.

Since 1967, the Machin portrait has appeared on all basic British definitive stamps. These have come in various formats, produced by different printing methods (basically gravure, intaglio and offset-litho) and by different printers. As such it has been estimated that it had been reproduced about 200 billion times by the time of its 40th anniversary, making it probably the most reproduced stamp image in history. Collectors recognise some 400 basic types (without simple phosphor variations) though whole books are required to catalogue all the minute differences. [1] The portrait has also been adapted for use on many types of British postal stationery, again with different printing techniques. Abroad, it has also been used on stamps, but normally as a small

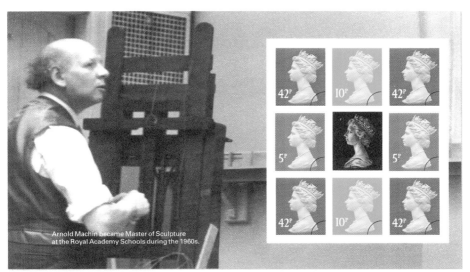

Proof of one of the stamp panes of the prestige stamp book featuring Machin at the Royal Academy Schools

cameo – though used fully on definitives of Hong Kong in 1992. Machin's simplified commemorative head has been used even more widely.

On the occasion of the 20th anniversary of the Machin head in 1987 I researched the genesis of the design for the first time and curated an exhibition at the then National Postal Museum in London. Arnold Machin visited the exhibition in the company of Sir Ron Dearing, Post Office Chairman, and I had the pleasure of taking them round, with Arnold posing for photographs in front of his old Kodak camera. Looking back I wonder at my innocence. Now, after 20 more years, I have found that there is still a great deal to be learnt. More official files have come to light and a lot more contemporary photographs and plaster casts or moulds. A re-evaluation, and reinterpretation, of these has brought a number of important new conclusions about what happened, and when, some 40 years ago. Some of these views as published here may yet be altered by new discoveries and there are still several holes in our knowledge at certain, crucial points.

5 June 2007.
Miniature sheet
celebrating the
40th anniversary of
the Machin design

Marking the anniversary

Apart from exhibitions and the publication of this book it is fitting that Royal Mail issue two new stamp designs (appearing in different formats) to mark the 40th anniversary of the Machin design in 2007. The designs feature a portrait of Arnold Machin on one and on the other his first, classic stamp in the colour particularly chosen by The Queen to emulate the Penny Black (a "stamp on stamp"). Various philatelic products accompany these, in particular a prestige stamp book containing the stamps and describing the design process in Arnold's own words (from *Picture to Post*). This is illustrated by a number of images described and shown in this book. Arnold would have been justly proud.

---

1   Those interested in the detail should consult: Myall, D.G.A. *The Complete Deegam Machin Handbook* Volumes 1 & 2, Third edition June 2003; *Stanley Gibbons Specialised Stamp Catalogue: Great Britain* Volumes 3 & 4 (2006); Skinner, J. *The Connoisseur Catalogue of Machin Stamps and Decimal Definitives* Tenth edition 1995 (supplement 2000); Machin Collectors Club *Specialised Machins Catalogue* 2004

A PERSONAL MEMOIR

BY FRANCIS MACHIN

Earliest recollections of my father are at our house in Stoke-on-Trent, a Victorian Italianate villa on an estate of some 20 such houses. They were built apparently for the more well-to-do pottery employees of the 19th century, but by then were very run-down. Less than a mile from his birthplace, he must have admired these houses in his youth. He installed his studio in the old greenhouse, complete with its Minton tiled floor,

Francis Machin, 2007

and this was very much his private domain. He whitewashed the windows to stop prying eyes, and as a small child, one had to be careful not to make too much noise on that side of the house – it was always something of a treat to be allowed in!

My father was dedicated to his work, but very patient also in helping me with various creative projects: a wooden pedal car, a den in the garden built from a pile of bricks, and a box of small wooden bricks used by kiln designers from which we made endless different constructions, the favourite being the tallest tower.

He captured my imagination in his modelling and design projects, and must have been adept at passing on his own enthusiasm. We made clay animals and fired them, hedgehogs being a favourite, as the spikes could be quickly made by pushing clay through a sieve.

In the house he installed a small kiln and I well remember the smell of firing that pervaded everywhere. He and my mother were embarked on a project to make ashtrays he'd designed, for which he could not find a manufacturer. They spent weeks moulding, drying, firing and glazing these, and apparently it was quite a commercial success from which they bought for the first time a new car – a peacock blue Citroën Light fifteen, of which my father was very proud. He was always making or doing something creative and rarely seemed to rest. From his weekly trips to London to teach he would arrive home with "Put the paper on the table" and out of some old cardboard box would produce a dusty collection of oil lamps, historic joinery tools, model steam engines, stuffed birds, or other relics he'd picked up in one of the many junk shops he would frequent between Stoke and London. Duly cleaned, examined, and if possible, restored to working order, these things found their way into my "museum".

I looked forward to his weekly return and the surprise it might bring, as he had an astute ability to see where my own interests lay, and to seek out things that might broaden it – a skill that no doubt greatly helped his students at the Royal College of Art and the Royal Academy. He was always interested in learning himself and picked up my new enthusiasms with equal relish. Once he had a commission to design a mosaic screen wall for a bar, and the interior of the swimming pool on the revolutionary liner Canberra, and took me on a trip to the Belfast shipyard. We went to look at the Giant's Causeway nearby, but most of his time was spent painstakingly ensuring that his designs were properly executed, while I sat in the design office, looking out of the window at the vast liner, watching an endless succession of ant-like men trailing up and down gangways carrying bits of equipment and tools.

One particular treat was to visit his old landlady, Tommy Thompson, in her terraced house where he had lodged in Derby. For a small boy it was a treasure trove of mystery. Tommy, elderly and frail, had never thrown anything away, and

had acquired many interesting relics and curios: ancient watches, boxes of minerals and fossils, tin toys. The dining room was largely taken up by a steel table, to shelter under during air raids in the war – now become a permanency along with piles and piles of newspapers stored under and on it. The temptation and excitement of these visits was enhanced by the possibility of acquiring one of these treasures. "Shall I give it him Arnold? Well shall I?", after longingly looking at or handling some old relic on countless occasions.

Architecture was of great interest to my father and on the way to see Tommy we drove past the greyhound track, behind a wall with a fine Doric portico which I think he must have drawn whilst a student at Derby Art School. We were always stopping on journeys to look at junk shops or buildings, churches being a favourite. Whilst he liked seclusion and quiet, he was more interested in the achievement of mankind than in raw nature. Although we went on many trips to look for fossils in the Peak District, visit abandoned watermills, I can't remember him going on a "country walk" even when we moved to live in a country cottage some 15 miles from Stoke-on-Trent. He was busy making his garden and putting his own mark on the landscape, sculpting the holly hedge with his shears, the old quarry face with hammer and chisel, and the grass with a ride-on lawnmower, making a labyrinth of paths through the head-high bracken.

Again, there, his sanctuary was his studio – this time a large prefabricated wooden shed raised on brick piers, perhaps to enhance the view across the valley, perhaps to ensure privacy, the windows being above eye-level from outside.

This was a busy period – Master of Sculpture at the Royal Academy, and commissions for the royal portraits on coins and stamps.

He kept me home from school one day to observe the new mains water pipe being installed by "mole-plough" across the field to our cottage. He thought it would be more educational, and certainly the memory of the intimate detail of the tractor, winch and straining steel cable pulling the blade through the earth with polythene pipe disappearing into the ground at the far side of the field has stuck with me, as has the previous routine of drawing water by hand from the deep well. Our move to the country was his gesture of returning closer to nature – we had no electricity for some time, relying on lamps and candles, but eventually he had to succumb to convenience.

In a great many ways he was ahead of his time – vegetarian, conscientious objector, opponent of the "urbanisation" of the landscape, of television and media, of mindless authority and conformity. He was a great believer in individuality, and stood firmly for his own beliefs.

Later, when I started my career in architecture and design he pursued his own interest in architectural motifs, creating designs in wrought iron, trelliswork, and building elaborate stone grottos. One was a huge construction which entailed the placing of 60 tons of enormous stones, using a mobile crane to make a subterranean tunnel, topped in an alcove above, with one of his sculptures of cherubs. He worked tirelessly on these ambitious projects well into his eighties.

We moved house when he was nearly 70, to a larger property where he started again on a new garden, wall building, designing cascades, waterfalls, and secret gardens. During this time he worked with my mother in the design of the metal trays for which she became well known, painting the gold decorated borders to her floral designs in the manner of his early years as a china painter at Mintons. He always enjoyed the commercial application of art and design, and was firmly of the belief that art and industry are inseparable.

He much enjoyed trips to France, with me and sometimes one of my children, to visit the semi-derelict farmhouse I was restoring there. "On holiday" he rarely rested; he would help rebuild a stone archway, or collect firewood, but he much enjoyed the journey and the thrill of new discoveries of churches, sculptures, cathedrals. We would often visit one particular church halfway from Calais where he marvelled at the effigies of a tomb, and spent many hours sketching and contemplating these works, picking up new ideas for the series of religious drawings he was producing at that time. Other favourite haunts were the cathedrals of Laon, Rheims, the abbey at Vezeley, but above all he enjoyed exploring the small forgotten churches where he would often quickly find some exquisite carving of an angel, or an interesting memorial. In fact, there was almost nowhere he would not root out something created, of interest, all of which he stored away and might use as reference in some future work.

One of his last projects was the dolls' house he designed and had built by his old student and friend, Peter Wall. This was for his grand-daughter Alice, and was started soon after her birth, being presented to her on her fifth birthday. Painstakingly detailed and executed, it incorporated all his passions in art and design. An elegant classical fronted brick building, sculptures, stained glass, pictures, furniture and a tiny envelope with his stamp faithfully reduced in miniature!

He always remembered the time he had spent at Barlaston (an ancient village in Staffordshire), being accommodated by the Wedgwoods so that he could progress his work in terracotta. Without their help and encouragement he might never have advanced from the pottery design he was engaged in. Later, he became very keen to create a similar facility for one or two able students where they could develop their ideas in an environment conducive to thought, reflection and creativity. Although the project commenced in his lifetime, it has only recently become operational, as a charitable organisation, The Machin Arts Foundation, created in memory of my parents, and to attempt to provide some continuity in the tradition of excellence in art and design they both subscribed to. A gallery has been made to house their lifetime's work, and several studios for students of figurative art are envisaged.

As he said in his memoirs: "Great artists go on experimenting because they have the vision and because they are inspired to help their fellows – I am reminded of D.H. Lawrence's words 'Things men have made with wakened hands, and breathed soft life into are awake through the years with transferred touch. For this reason some old things are lovely, warm still with the lives of forgotten men who made them.'"

INDEX

ILLUSTRATION ACKNOWLEDGEMENTS

All illustrations are © Royal Mail Group 2007 unless otherwise stated
(as listed here).

Page

1   David Gentleman *Zac Macaulay*

9   Drawing by Henry Corbould *H M The Queen*

     Penny Black experimental proofs
     *Philatelic Archives, Museumsstiftung Post und
     Telekommunikation, Bonn (Germany)*

21-7 *Machin Art Foundation*

32   Royal Mint Advisory Committee minutes
      Royal Mint

40   Sketch *Machin Art Foundation*

42   Wax effigy and original plaster cast
      Machin Art Foundation

43   Royal Mint Advisory Committee minutes
      Royal Mint

44   Royal Mint Advisory Committee minutes
      Royal Mint

45   Drawing from life *Machin Art Foundation*

47   Original mould *Machin Art Foundation*

48   Plaster cast and metal matrix *Royal Mint*

49   Royal Mint Advisory Committee minutes *Royal
      Mint*

50   Original mould *Machin Art Foundation*

51   Royal Mint Advisory Committee minutes
      Royal Mint

52   Royal Mint punch and proof 10p coin
      Royal Mint

79   Gillick plaster cast *Royal Mint*

80   Gentleman woodblock *David Gentleman*

125   Machin portrait rendering [top]
      Machin Art Foundation

126   Penny Black sketch [bottom left]
      Machin Art Foundation

127   Machin sketch [top right]
      Machin Art Foundation

133   Photograph of coin mould
      Machin Art Foundation

134   Worked photographs of coin mould
      Machin Art Foundation

135   Photograph of plaster mould
      Machin Art Foundation

136   Photographs of cast and mould
      Machin Art Foundation

138-9 Photographs of moulds and first cast
       Machin Art Foundation

140   Machin sketch *Machin Art Foundation*

145   Photographic simplification
      Machin Art Foundation

158   Diadem *H. M. The Queen*

159   Plaster mould *Machin Art Foundation*

162   Plaster mould *Machin Art Foundation*

176   Approved card *H. M. The Queen*

188   High value sketches *Machin Art Foundation*

190-1 Plaster cast photographs
       Machin Art Foundation

200   Photographic sketch *Machin Art Foundation*

203   Electrotype *Royal Mint*

222   Jeffery Matthews *Smack*

227-32 *Machin Art Foundation*